1000 things you should know about

sharks

Anna Claybourne

MiLeS
KeLLy
PUBLISHING

This material was first published as hardback in 2004

This edition published in 2006 by Miles Kelly Publishing Ltd
Bardfield Centre, Great Bardfield, Essex, CM7 4SL

2 4 6 8 10 9 7 5 3 1

Editorial Director: Belinda Gallagher
Art Director: Jo Brewer
Editor: Rosalind McGuire
Volume Designer: Ian Paulyn
Additional Design: Candice Bekir
Picture Researcher: Liberty Newton
Reprographics: Anthony Cambray, Mike Coupe,
Stephan Davis, Ian Paulyn

British Library Cataloguing-in-Publication Data
A catalogue record for this book is available from the British Library

ISBN 1-84236-688-2

Printed in China

info@mileskelly.net
www.mileskelly.net

All artworks from the MKP Archives

The publishers would like to thank the following sources for the use
of their photographs:
Page 49 Universal/pictorialpress.com, Page 58 Warner/pictorialpress.com

All photographs from:
Castrol, CMCD, Corbis, Corel, digitalSTOCK, digitalvision, Flat Earth,
Hemera, ILN, John Foxx, PhotoAlto, PhotoDisc, PhotoEssentials,
PhotoPro, Stockbyte

CONTENTS

SHARK ANATOMY   6–13

All about sharks 6
Shark shapes 6
Shark sizes 7
Inside a shark 8
Bendy bones 8

Shark skin 9
Tails and fins 9
Spikes and spines 10
Shark vision 10
Sensing sounds 11

Touch and taste 11
Sensing smells 12
The sixth sense 13
Smart sharks 13

HOW SHARKS LIVE   14–25

How sharks breathe 14
How sharks swim 14
Shark teeth 15
What sharks eat 16
How sharks hunt 16
Filter-feeding 17
Scavenging 17

Lighting up 18
Staying safe 18
Sharks in disguise 19
Loners and groups 19
Meeting and mating 20
Communication 21
Shark eggs 21

Shark young 22
Growing up 22
Shark companions 23
Where sharks live 24
Sharks at home 24
Long-distance travel 25

SHARK SPECIES   25–48

Types of shark 25
Great white sharks 26
Mako sharks 26
Thresher sharks 27
Sandtiger sharks 28
Porbeagle sharks 28
Basking sharks 29
Goblin sharks 29
Crocodile sharks 30
Megamouth sharks 30
Tiger sharks 31
Bull sharks 32
Blue sharks 32
White-tip sharks 33

Black-tip sharks 33
Bonnethead sharks 34
Hammerhead sharks 35
Lemon sharks 35
Houndsharks 36
Weasel sharks and catsharks 36
Dogfish sharks 37
Greenland sharks 37
Dwarf and pygmy sharks 38
Prickly and bramble sharks 38
Cookie-cutter sharks 39
Carpet sharks 40
Wobbegongs 40
Nurse sharks 41

Blind sharks 41
Tawny and zebra sharks 42
Whale sharks 42
Hornsharks 43
Angel sharks 43
Saw sharks 44
Frilled sharks 45
Shark relatives 45
Rays 46
Types of rays 46
Sawfish 47
Skates 47
Chimaeras 48

SHARKS AND PEOPLE   48–58

Sharks and humans 48
Fear of sharks 49
Shark attacks 49
Survival stories 50
Shark safety 51
Dangerous sharks 51

Harmless sharks 52
Shark fishing 52
Sharks as food 53
More uses for sharks 53
Shark tourism 54
Sharks in captivity 54

Sharks in trouble 55
Endangered species 55
Shark beliefs and folklore 56
Shark myths and legends 56
Saving sharks 57
Sharks in art, books and films 58

SHARK SCIENCE   58–61

Shark science 58
Shark scientists 59
Studying sharks 59

Early sharks 60
Shark fossils 60
Shark discoveries and mysteries . . .61

Shark records 61

INDEX   62

All about sharks

- **Sharks are a type of fish.** They live and breathe underwater and are brilliant swimmers.

- **All sharks are carnivores,** which means they eat other animals. Many are fierce hunters.

- **Sharks are found in seas and oceans** and in a few rivers too.

- **There are about** 400 different species of shark.

- **A species is the name for a particular type of shark** or other living thing. Sharks of the same species can mate and have young.

- **Most sharks have long bodies,** triangle-shaped fins and lots of sharp teeth.

◄ *A great white shark on the prowl. Many sharks hunt and eat other types of fish, as well as all kinds of sea creatures.*

- **Sharks range in size** from about the size of a banana to bigger than a bus.

- **Sharks are closely related to other fish called rays** and skates. They are similar to sharks but usually have much flatter bodies.

- **Sharks have existed** for almost 400 million years.

- **Most sharks are not dangerous.** Only a few species have been known to attack humans.

Shark shapes

- **A typical shark** has a long, narrow, torpedo-shaped body, designed for moving quickly through the water.

- **All sharks,** even unusually shaped ones, have the same basic body parts: a head with eyes, nostrils and a mouth, a body, a tail and fins.

- **A body shape designed for speed,** like a shark's, is called a 'streamlined' shape. It allows water to move past it easily with very little resistance or 'drag'.

- **The tip of a shark's nose** is called the snout. Most sharks' snouts are pointed, like the tip of a bullet.

- **A shark's mouth** is usually a long way back underneath its snout.

> **★ STAR FACT ★**
> Some sharks can change shape. Swell sharks inflate their bodies with water or air to make themselves bigger and rounder.

- **Hammerhead sharks** get their name because their heads are shaped like wide, flat hammers.

- **Angel sharks** have wide, spread-out fins that look like an angel's wings.

- **Engineers sometimes study** sharks' fins and bodies to determine the best shapes for aeroplane wings or boat hulls.

- **Some large fish,** such as tuna, are shaped like sharks.

◄ *Due to the strange shape of their heads, hammerhead sharks are probably the easiest to recognize of all sharks.*

Shark sizes

◄ Although sharks vary greatly in size, most of them have similar torpedo-shaped bodies that enable them to cut through water at speed.

- **The whale shark** is the biggest living shark. It can reach a maximum size of 18 m – as long as two buses end-to-end.

- **The biggest shark ever**, *Megalodon*, is now extinct. Scientists think it may have weighed almost twice as much a whale shark.

- **The biggest sharks** are gentle creatures that filter tiny food particles from the water.

- **The biggest hunting shark** is the great white shark.

- **A great white shark's mouth** can measure up to 40 cm across.

- **Most sharks are medium-sized**, measuring between 1 m and 3 m in length.

- **The smallest sharks** are the spined pygmy shark and the dwarf lanternshark. They would fit on two pages of this book.

- **The average size for a shark** is very similar to the size of a human.

- **Although some sharks are small**, most are bigger than other types of fish.

- **Sharks aren't the biggest animals in the sea.** Some whales are bigger – but they are mammals, not fish.

▲ This is a whale shark, the biggest shark of all. It swims along with its mouth wide open in order to collect food from the water.

Inside a shark

- **Sharks are vertebrates** – they have a skeleton with a backbone. Many types of animals, including all fish, reptiles, birds and mammals, are vertebrates.

- **Sharks' skeletons** are not made of bone, but of cartilage (see bendy bones).

- **Sharks have thick layers of muscles** just under their skin. They are used to move the body from side to side as it swims.

- **Most of a shark's vital organs** are in a cavity in the middle of its body. Sharks have many of the same organs as other animals.

- **Sharks' livers** contain a lot of oil. Oil is lighter than water, so this helps it to float.

- **A shark's stomach is stretchy.** It can expand so that the shark can consume large amounts of food quickly.

- **Just like humans,** sharks have a heart that pumps blood around their bodies.

- **Most sharks are cold-blooded,** which means their blood is the same temperature as the water around them.

- **A few sharks are warm-blooded** – they can heat their blood to be warmer than their surroundings. This helps them to swim faster and move into cooler water to hunt.

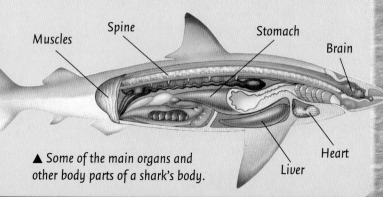

Muscles Spine Stomach Brain Heart Liver

▲ Some of the main organs and other body parts of a shark's body.

Bendy bones

- **Cartilage** is the white or pale blue, rubbery, bendy substance that sharks' skeletons are made of.

- **A shark's bendy skeleton** gives it flexibility, helping it to twist and turn in the water.

- **Although human skeletons** are made of bone, they have a small amount of cartilage too. It can be felt in the bendy tip of the nose.

- **Cartilage can also be found in meat.** It's the tough, chewy substance that's usually called 'gristle'.

- **As well as being very flexible,** cartilage is lighter than bone, giving sharks lots of strength without making them heavy.

- **Most other fish have bones** instead of cartilage. They are called 'bony fish', while sharks, rays and skates are known as 'cartilaginous fish'.

- **Sharks' fins and tails** contain hundreds of thin rods of cartilage, which stiffen them and give them their shape.

- **A shark's spine and skull** are harder than the rest of its skeleton. They need to be stronger to hold the body together and protect the brain.

- **Sharks have simpler skeletons** than most other bony fish, with fewer ribs and other parts.

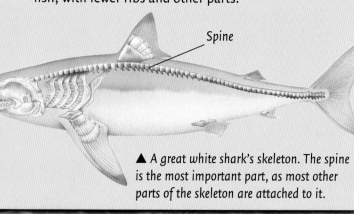

Spine

▲ A great white shark's skeleton. The spine is the most important part, as most other parts of the skeleton are attached to it.

Shark skin

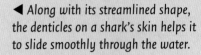

- **Sharks don't have scales,** like other fish. Instead their skin is covered with tiny, hard points called denticles.

- **The word 'denticle' means 'little tooth'** – because denticles are very similar to teeth.

- **Denticles make a shark's skin** feel very rough to the touch. Some swimmers have been badly scratched just from brushing against a shark.

- **Denticles have two uses:** they protect the shark from enemies and help it to slide through the water.

- **Denticles range** from microscopic in size to about 5 mm across.

- **The shape of denticles varies** on different parts of a shark's body, and from one shark species to another.

◀ Along with its streamlined shape, the denticles on a shark's skin helps it to slide smoothly through the water.

- **Denticles on the side** of a shark are the sharpest – ensuring fast movement through the water.

- **Sharks also release** a slimy substance from their skin, to make their bodies move through the water even faster.

- **Large sharks have very thick skin** – thicker than a human finger.

★ STAR FACT ★
Shark skin is so rough that in the past it was used to make a type of sandpaper, called shagreen.

Tails and fins

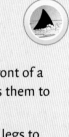

- **A typical shark** has up to seven fins, not including its tail. Fins help sharks to swim and cut through water.

- **The big fin on a shark's back** is called the dorsal fin. It's the one that can be seen sticking out of the water in shark films. A shark's dorsal fin stops its body swinging from side to side while swimming.

- **A shark's tail** is also known as its 'caudal fin'. The anal fin is just in front of the tail.

- **A shark's tail is made up of** two points called lobes – an upper lobe and a lower lobe.

- **There are two large pectoral fins** near the front of a shark's body, a bit like arms. The shark uses them to steer while swimming.

- **Epaulette sharks** use their pectoral fins like legs to 'crawl' along the seabed.

- **In parts of Asia**, people use sharks' fins to make a special kind of soup.

- **Thresher sharks** can be recognized by their very long upper tail lobes.

- **A whale shark's pectoral fin** can be a massive 2 m long – that's as big as a bed!

★ STAR FACT ★
Without their fins, sharks wouldn't be able to stay the right way up. They would roll over in the water.

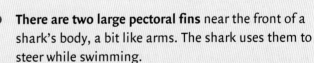

Anal fin

Dorsal fin

Pectoral fin

◀ Hammerhead sharks have very long dorsal fins.

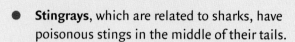

Spikes and spines

- **Many prehistoric sharks** had sharp spines in front of their dorsal fins. Scientists think these may have helped to hold the fins up.

- **Today,** only a few sharks have spines, spikes or sharp horns on their bodies. They usually use them to fight off attackers.

- **Some dogfish sharks** and horn sharks have two sharp 'fin spines' in front of their dorsal fins, which can inflict a painful wound.

- **The spined pygmy shark** is the only shark that has just one spine, not two or none.

- **Stingrays**, which are related to sharks, have poisonous stings in the middle of their tails.

- **Smaller sharks** are more likely to have spines. They are most at risk of being eaten, so they need defences that will deter their enemies from biting them.

- **Spiny dogfish** coil themselves right around their enemies to stab them with their spines.

- **Shark spines** are made of modified, extra-large denticles.

- **Saw sharks** have long, saw-shaped snouts, edged with sharp teeth.

- **A sawfish** is a type of ray, and is closely related to sharks. Its sharp, spiky snout can grow to almost 2 m long.

◄ *Saw sharks have small, sharp spikes along their long snouts. They use their snouts to slash at fish or to dig for prey in the seabed.*

Shark vision

- **Most sharks** have big eyes and good eyesight. They mainly use it to spot their prey.

- **Sharks need to be able to see well** in the dark, as there is limited light underwater.

- **Many sharks** have a layer called the *tapetum lucidum* at the back of their eyes. It collects and reflects light, helping them to see, even in the gloomy darkness.

- **The *tapetum lucidum*** (Latin for 'bright carpet') makes sharks' eyes appear to glow in the dark.

- **Some sharks** have slit-shaped pupils, like a cat's.

- **Scientists think** sharks can probably see in colour.

- **Some very deepwater sharks** have small eyes and poor eyesight. The deepest oceans are so dark, many animals living there rely on other senses instead.

- **Sharks have a third eye**, called a pineal eye, under the skin in their foreheads. It can't see as well as a normal eye, but it can sense daylight.

> ★ **STAR FACT** ★
> Most sharks never close their eyes. Some have special see-through eyelids that protect their eyes without cutting out any light. Others just roll their eyes up into their head to protect them.

- **The shy-eye shark** gets its name because when it is caught, it covers its eyes with its tail to shield them from the light.

▶ *A close-up of a tiger shark's eye, showing a special eyelid called the nictitating membrane. This closes over the eye when the shark is about to bite, to protect it from being damaged.*

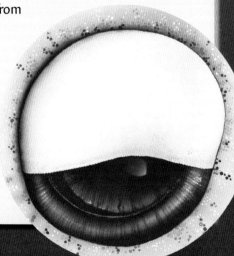

Sensing sounds

- **Sharks have ears**, but they're very hard to spot. Their openings are nothing more than tiny holes, just behind the shark's eyes.

- **If you think you can see a shark's ears**, you're probably looking at its spiracles, which can look a bit like ears, but are in fact used for breathing.

- **In the sea**, sound travels in the form of vibrations rippling through the water. Sharks hear by sensing these vibrations.

- **Inside a shark's ear** is a set of looping, fluid-filled tubes called the 'labyrinth'.

- **Sharks hear** using tiny microscopic hairs inside the labyrinth. Vibrations travel through the fluid, moving the hairs, which send signals to the shark's brain.

◄ Scientists and tourists sometimes use cages to safely get close to sharks.

- **A shark's hearing** is its best long-distance sense. Some sharks can hear sounds from several kilometres away.

- **Sharks are best at hearing low sounds**, such as the noise made by an injured animal underwater.

> ★ STAR FACT ★
> Although sharks can hear sounds, they rarely make a noise.

- **Ears also help sharks** to keep their balance. Movements of the fluid inside their ears tell them which way up they are.

- **Some sharks can recognize** the clanking sound of shark-watching cages. When they hear it, sharks may try to find the cages, in the hope of being fed.

Touch and taste

- **Like us**, sharks can feel things that touch their skin. They can also feel things that are nearby, from the ripples they make as water flows around them.

- **Like humans**, sharks have nerve endings all over their skin that can feel pressure, temperature and pain.

- **Sharks also have an extra sense organ** called the 'lateral line'. This is a long tube running down each side of a shark's body, under its skin.

- **As a shark swims**, ripples in the water pass into the lateral line through tiny holes in the skin. Hairs inside the lateral line sense the ripples, and send signals to the shark's brain.

- **All fish**, not just sharks, have lateral lines.

> ★ STAR FACT ★
> A shark can sense a turtle, octopus or other prey from up to 20 m away.

- **Sharks use their sense of touch** to navigate. They can 'feel' where obstacles are, even if they can't see them.

- **Sharks have taste buds** inside their mouths.

- **As well as tasting the food they eat**, sharks can taste chemicals dissolved in the water. This helps them to find prey and avoid pollution.

- **Some sharks have fleshy 'whiskers'** on their snouts, called barbels. These can sense the location of food on the seabed.

The lateral line

◄ The lateral line runs down the side of the shark's body, from its gills to its tail.

Sensing smells

- **The sense of smell** is the most important sense for most sharks.

- **As a shark swims**, water constantly flows into the nostrils on its snout, and over the scent-detecting cells inside them.

- **Sharks can smell blood in water**, even if it's diluted to one part in ten million. That's like one drop of blood mixed into a small swimming pool.

- **A shark can smell an injured animal** up to 1 km away.

- **The biggest part of a shark's brain** is the olfactory lobe – the part used for processing smells.

- **The great white shark** has biggest olfactory lobe of all – which means it probably has the best sense of smell of any shark.

- **Swimmers have been known to attract sharks** just by having a tiny scratch on their skin.

- **Sharks use their nostrils** for smelling, not breathing.

- **A shark homes in on a scent** by zig-zagging its snout from side to side. It moves towards the side where the smell is strongest.

▼ *A great white shark hunting, trying to detect traces of blood from injured fish or other animals. The water flows into the nostrils at the front of its snout as it swims along.*

> **★ STAR FACT ★**
> In one experiment, a scientist plugged a shark's nostril. It swam around in a circle!

The sixth sense

- **A shark has six senses**. Besides vision, hearing, touch, taste and smell, sharks can also sense the tiny amounts of electricity given off by other animals.

- **To detect electricity**, a shark has tiny holes in the skin around its head and snout. They're called the 'ampullae of Lorenzini'.

- **Ampullae** are a type of Roman bottle. The ampullae of Lorenzini get their name because of their narrow-necked bottle shape.

- **Each ampulla** contains a jelly-like substance, which collects electric signals.

- **All animals** give off tiny amounts of electricity when their muscles move. Electricity doesn't travel well through air, but it travels well through water.

- **A shark's ampullae of Lorenzini** can sense animals within a range of about one metre.

- **Some sharks** use their electrical sense to find prey that's buried in the seabed.

- **A fierce hunting shark** such as a tiger shark has up to 1500 ampullae of Lorenzini.

- **Stefano Lorenzini** was an Italian anatomist (body scientist) who studied the ampullae of Lorenzini.

◀ *Each ampulla looks like a tiny hole. Beneath the surface of the skin it opens into a wider bottle shape.*

Smart sharks

- **Most sharks** have big brains for their body size and are probably smarter than many bony fish.

- **Almost all of a shark's brain** is used for processing information from the senses.

- **The brain parts** used for learning and thinking are quite small in sharks.

- **In relation to their body size**, hammerhead sharks have the biggest brains.

- **In captivity**, some sharks have learned to do simple tasks in exchange for a reward.

- **Experiments with lemon sharks** show they can recognize different shapes and colours.

- **Some sharks are brighter than others**. Fast hunters such as great whites are the most intelligent. Slow-moving bottom-feeders like carpet sharks are less smart.

- **Scientists used to think** all sharks had little intelligence. They have only recently started to learn about how their brains work.

- **Sharks can be trained** to fetch rubber rings, just like a dog fetching a stick.

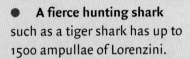

◀ *A scalloped hammerhead, one of the smartest sharks. Hammerhead sharks are fast, fierce hunters. They also spend time in groups and scientists think they have simple social systems.*

How sharks breathe

- **Like most animals**, sharks need to take in oxygen to make their bodies work.

- **Like other fish**, sharks breathe underwater using gills in their throats.

- **Most sharks have five pairs of gills.** Each gill is made up of a set of hair-like filaments full of blood vessels.

- **Many sharks have extra breathing holes** called spiracles, just behind their eyes, that take in water for the shark to breathe.

- **Sharks do not have lungs** – their gills do the same job that lungs do in humans.

- **As a shark swims**, water flows into its spiracles or mouth and past the gills, where oxygen is taken out of the water into the shark's bloodstream.

- **The water flows out again through the gill slits** – the lines you can see on the sides of a shark's neck.

★ STAR FACT ★
Sea water contains just one percent oxygen gas – much less than air, which is 21 percent oxygen.

◀ *The five gill slits on this silky shark's throat are clearly visible.*

- **Some fast sharks**, such as mako sharks, have to swim continuously so that water flows over their gills and they can breathe. If they stop, water stops flowing past their gills and they suffocate.

- **Slow-moving sharks** such as the Port Jackson shark are able to pump water across their gills using the muscles of their mouth and neck, so they can stop for a rest and still keep breathing.

How sharks swim

★ STAR FACT ★
If sharks don't keep swimming, they gradually sink onto the seabed.

- **A shark's main swimming organ** is its tail. A shark thrashes its tail to push itself through the water.

- **Sharks use their pectoral and pelvic fins** to help them steer and swim upwards and downwards.

- **The fastest shark** is the shortfin mako shark, which has been recorded swimming at over 55 km/hour.

- **Most sharks** have an everyday cruising speed of around 8 km/hour.

- **Sharks normally swim** with a regular rhythm. They don't dart around like most bony fish do.

- **Other bony fish** have a swim bladder – a gas-filled organ that keeps them afloat. Sharks don't have swim bladders, so they are slightly heavier than water.

- **Many sharks swim** in a figure-of-eight pattern when they are annoyed.

- **Sharks are streamlined** so they can swim very quietly.

- **Some sharks swallow air** to help them to float better.

▶ *White-tip reef sharks often stop swimming to rest on the seabed. As they are heavier than water, they have to start swimming again if they want to move off the seabed.*

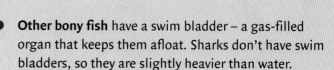

Shark teeth

★ STAR FACT ★
A typical shark has several hundred
teeth at any one time.

- **A hunting shark,** such as a great white or a tiger shark, has several rows of teeth.

- **A shark's gums** are like a conveyor belt. The rows of teeth constantly move slowly forwards. Gradually the front row wears out, and a new row replaces them.

- **Only the two front rows of teeth** are used for biting. The rest are just lining up to replace them.

- **In a lifetime,** some sharks will get through 30,000 teeth altogether.

▲ A great white shark stretches its mouth wide open, revealing its sharp, triangle-shaped teeth.

- **You can sometimes find** sharks' old, used teeth washed up on beaches.

- **Shark's teeth** really are as sharp as razors. Each tooth has serrated edges, with tiny, sharp points on them, like a saw, for cutting through meat.

- **The biggest shark teeth** belong to the great white shark. They can grow to over 6 cm long.

- **Some sharks,** such as smooth-houndsharks, don't have sharp biting teeth. Instead they have hard, flat plates in their mouths for grinding up crabs and shellfish.

- **The sand tiger shark** has the deadliest-looking teeth – but they are only used for catching small fish.

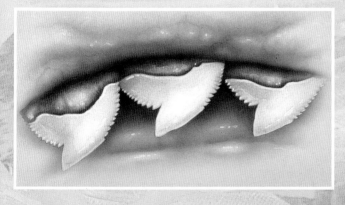

◀ A tiger shark's teeth have very sharp, serrated edges, like a sharp knife. This helps the teeth to cut through flesh.

What sharks eat

- **Most sharks** eat many different kinds of animals.

- **Big, fast hunting sharks**, such as great whites and bull sharks, feed on large fish (including other sharks), as well as seals, turtles, octopuses, squid, seabirds and other sea creatures.

- **Many smaller sharks**, such as dogfish sharks, hunt smaller fish, octopuses and squid.

- **Slow-moving sharks**, such as nurse sharks, angel sharks and carpet sharks, crunch up crabs, shrimps and shellfish that they find on the seabed.

▼ Hammerhead sharks prey on other sharks, rays, bony fish, crabs and lobsters, octopuses and squid.

- **Filter-feeders** are sharks that feed on plankton – tiny floating animals and plants – which they filter out of the water.

- **There are hardly any animal species** in the sea that aren't part of the diet of one shark or another.

- **Tiger sharks are well-known for eating anything** they can find, including objects that aren't food, such as tin cans.

- **After being eaten**, food stays in a shark's stomach for up to three days.

- **Most sharks don't eat every day**. Some big hunters can go without food for months.

> **★ STAR FACT ★**
> Sharks generally prefer the taste of fish, seals and turtles to the taste of humans.

How sharks hunt

- **Most sharks are nocturnal** – which means they hunt at night, or crepuscular – which means they hunt at dusk.

- **Before attacking**, some sharks 'bump' their prey with their snouts, probably to see if it's something edible.

- **When about to bite**, a shark raises its snout and thrusts its jaws forward, so that its teeth stick out.

- **Some sharks shake their prey** from side to side to rip it apart.

- **Sharks don't usually chew** – they tear their prey into chunks or just swallow it whole.

- **Some sharks will attack** animals that are much bigger than themselves.

- **Sometimes**, lots of sharks are attracted to a source of food, and they all jostle to eat it at the same time. This is known as a 'feeding frenzy'.

◀ This great white is taking a bite out of a piece of meat dangled from a boat. Although it isn't hunting, you can see it is thrusting its teeth forward to attack.

- **Most hunting sharks** prefer prey that's weak or helpless, because it's easier to catch. That's why sharks are good at smelling blood – it tells them when an animal is injured.

- **Many sharks give their prey a fatal bite**, then leave it to bleed to death. They then return to feed on the body.

> **★ STAR FACT ★**
> Sharks have very strong jaws. They can bite other animals in half – even those with tough shell, such as turtles.

Filter-feeding

- **The biggest sharks of all** – whale sharks, basking sharks and megamouths – eat the smallest prey – plankton. These sharks are the filter-feeders.

- **Plankton** is made up of small sea creatures such as shrimps, baby crabs and squid, little fish and tiny free-floating plants. It drifts along with the currents.

- **Filter-feeding sharks** have 'gill rakers'. These are special comblike bristles in their throats that sieve plankton out of the water.

- **Gill rakers** are coated in sticky mucus to help plankton to stick to them.

- **Filter-feeding sharks swallow the plankton** they have collected, while the water they have sieved escapes from their gills.

Plankton

◄ Whale sharks are filter-feeders. Although they are huge, they feed on some of the tiniest animals in the sea – plankton.

- **Filter-feeders have massive mouths** so they can suck in as much water as possible.

- **To collect a kilogram of plankton,** a shark has to filter one million litres of water.

- **In one hour,** a whale shark filters around 2 million litres of water, and collects 2 kg of food.

- **Whale sharks** sometimes suck in shoals of little fish, such as sardines, that are also busy feeding on plankton.

- **Some other big sea creatures** – such as the blue whale, the world's biggest animal – are also filter-feeders.

Scavenging

> ★ **STAR FACT** ★
> In Australia in 1935, a tiger shark vomited up a human arm. The shark had not killed anyone but had scavenged the arm after a murder victim had been cut up with a knife and thrown into the sea.

- **Scavenging** means feeding on other hunters' leftovers or on animals that are dying or already dead.

- **Almost all sharks** will scavenge if they can't find other food.

- **Some sharks,** such as the Greenland shark and the smooth dogfish, get a lot of their food by scavenging.

- **Sharks in deep water** often feed on dead sea creatures that sink down from higher levels.

- **Sharks are much more likely to eat people** who have already drowned than they are to attack living people.

- **Sharks scavenge humans' food too** – especially waste food that's thrown overboard from ships.

- **Sharks sometimes eat fish** caught in fishing boats' nets before they can be pulled to the surface.

- **Great white sharks love to scavenge** – especially on the bodies of dead whales.

- **Scavenging is kind of natural recycling.** It keeps the oceans clean, and makes sure leftovers and dead animals are rapidly recycled rather than left to slowly decompose.

◄ Sharkwatchers make use of the great white's scavenging behaviour, drawing it close to their boat using a chunk of meat attached to a line.

Lighting up

- **Some sharks** can glow in the dark.

- **When animals give off light**, it's known as bioluminescence, which means 'living light'.

- **Glowing sharks** are often found in the deepest, darkest oceans.

- **Some deep-sea glowing sharks**, such as the velvet belly shark, may use their lights to illuminate their surroundings and help them see their prey.

- **Lanternsharks** have glowing dots around and inside their mouths. This may attract small fish and lure them into the shark's mouth.

- **Some sharks that live at medium depths** have glowing undersides. This makes them hard to see from below, as their light bellies match the light coming down from the sea surface.

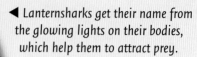

◄ *Lanternsharks get their name from the glowing lights on their bodies, which help them to attract prey.*

- **Sharks may use bioluminescence to communicate.** For example, green dogfish sharks feed in groups. Their light patterns may help them to find each other.

- **Glowing lights** may also help sharks to find a mate of their own species in the darkness of the deep ocean.

- **Bioluminescence** is made in tiny organs in the skin called 'photophores'. In a photophore, two chemicals are combined, creating a reaction that gives off light.

- **Some other animals** have bioluminescence too. They include deep sea fish such as the anglerfish, as well as fireflies and some types of worms.

Staying safe

- **Smaller sharks** make a tasty snack for other animals, so they need to defend themselves against predators such as killer whales, dolphins and porpoises.

- **The biggest sharks are rarely eaten** by other sea creatures, but they can still be hunted by humans.

- **Sharks are good at hiding.** They slip in between rocks, or into caves to escape from their enemies.

- **When in danger**, some sharks swim in a jerky, random manner to confuse their attacker.

- **Thresher sharks** use their tails to fight off predators, as well as for attacking their own prey.

★ **STAR FACT** ★
As another way to put off attackers, sharks can turn their stomachs inside out and vomit up their latest meal. Some predators eat the vomit instead of the shark.

- **Swell sharks** can inflate their bodies while in a small space between rocks. This wedges the shark into the space so that it can't be pulled out by a predator.

- **Sharks' skin** acts like armour, making it hard for predators to bite them.

- **Sharks with spines** can often put a predator off by giving it a sharp stab.

- **Most sharks are scared of humans.** If they hear divers, they will usually swim away quickly.

◄ *When great whites feel threatened, they open their mouths wide to show off their sharp teeth.*

Sharks in disguise

- **Many sharks** can disguise themselves to look like their surroundings. This is called 'camouflage'.

- **Camouflage** is a good way to hide from enemies, but it can also be used to help sharks sneak up on their prey without being seen.

- **Many small sharks**, such as zebra sharks, epaulette sharks and wobbegongs, have brown or grey patterns to help them blend in with coral and seaweed.

- **Sharks are often darker** on their top half and paler on their bottom half. This is called countershading.

- **A shark with countershading** viewed from below will blend with the brightly lit sea surface. Seen from above, it blends with the murky depths.

- **Some wobbegong sharks** have barbels that look like seaweed around their mouths. The fake seaweed tricks fish to come close so the wobbegong can catch them.

- **Angel sharks** have very flat, smooth bodies. When they lie on the sandy seabed they become almost invisible.

- **The shovelnose shark** or guitarfish (really a type of ray) disguises itself by burying itself under the seabed, with only its eyes sticking out.

- **The cookie-cutter shark** uses patches of light on its skin to attract hunting fish, seals or whales to come close – then the cookie-cutter takes a bite out of them.

- **When leopard sharks are young**, they have spots to help them hide. As they get older and bigger they don't need so much protection, and the spots fade.

◄ A silvertip shark demonstrates the countershading that many sharks have – pale skin on the underside, and darker skin above.

Loners and groups

- **Many sharks**, such as whale sharks and bull sharks, are solitary. This means that they like to live alone.

- **Sharks don't live in families**. They meet up to mate, but a mating pair do not live together. Their young do not live with them either.

- **Some sharks form groups** with other members of their species. White-tip reef sharks, for example, often rest together in small groups of about ten individuals.

- **Sharks may form groups** because there's safety in numbers. A group of sharks are less likely to be attacked than a single shark.

- **Hammerhead sharks** prefer to live in groups. They travel in shoals of hundreds of sharks.

★ **STAR FACT** ★
Groups of nurse sharks sometimes relax by lying in a heap on the seabed.

- **Being in a group** may help sharks to find a mate.

- **Some species**, such as lemon sharks, form single-sex groups of just males or just females. Scientists are not sure why.

- **Porbeagle sharks** have been seen playing together in groups of about 20.

- **Great whites** are usually solitary, but scientists have found that they sometimes hunt in pairs.

◄ Hammerheads are happy to spend time swimming together in huge shoals.

Meeting and mating

- **Like most animals**, sharks have to mate in order to reproduce.

- **Mating happens** when a male and a female of the same species meet up, and the male gives the female some cells from his body. This allows her to make new young inside her body.

- **Nurse sharks**, blue sharks and many other species have special mating areas in shallow parts of the sea.

- **In other species**, such as white-tip reef sharks, the females release pheromones to help the males find them.

- **Male sharks** sometimes bite female sharks to show they want to mate with them.

▼ *Male white-tip reef sharks sometimes spend time resting in shallow water during the day. If they smell a pheromone scent from a female telling them she's looking for a mate, they will try to find her.*

★ STAR FACT ★
The ancient Greek scientist and writer Aristotle studied and wrote about how sharks mate over 2300 years ago.

- **Female sharks** often have thicker skin than males so that being bitten during courtship doesn't harm them.

- **When sharks mate**, the male uses two body parts called claspers to deliver cells into an opening in the female's body, called the cloaca.

- **Sharks often wind their bodies** around each other when they are mating.

- **Sharks don't mate very often**. In most species, they only reproduce only once every two years.

Communication

- **Animals don't have complicated languages** like humans do – but they can still communicate.

- **When they are close together**, sharks can 'talk' using body language. They make different postures, just as humans show their feelings by making faces.

- **For example**, when a shark is annoyed or frightened, it arches its back, raises its snout, and points its pectoral fins down.

- **Sharks also release special scents** called pheromones to send messages to other sharks. These can indicate if a shark is looking for a mate or feeling agitated.

- **Many other animals use pheromones too**, including moths, bees, pigs, deer, and humans.

> ★ STAR FACT ★
> One shark kept in captivity could detect the minute electrical current caused by corroding metal near its tank.

- **When sharks live in a group**, the strongest ones usually become the leaders. They will sometimes have fights with the other sharks to show their dominance.

- **Bioluminescence** (lighting up) helps some sharks to communicate. It can help a shark recognize another shark of the same species in the dark.

- **Sharks may also be able to recognize each other** from the ripples their bodies make as they swim.

- **A few shark species** can make sounds. Swell sharks can make a barking noise, but experts are not sure if it's a way of 'talking'.

◀ *This shark is displaying aggression. Its raised snout, arched back and lowered fins mean it's ready to attack.*

Shark eggs

- **Many sharks** have young by laying eggs, as most bony fish do. Sharks that do this are called 'oviparous' sharks.

- **Bullhead**, dogfish, horn, zebra and swell sharks are all oviparous sharks.

- **A typical shark** lays between 10 and 20 eggs at a time.

- **A mother shark** doesn't guard her eggs. She lays them in a safe place, such as between two rocks or under a clump of seaweed, then leaves them to hatch.

- **Sharks' eggs** are enclosed in protective egg cases. The egg cases come in many shapes, including tubes, spirals and pillow shapes.

> ★ STAR FACT ★
> Catsharks' eggs have sticky strings on them that wind around seaweed, holding the eggs secure.

- **When the female first lays her eggs**, their cases are soft, but when they come in contact with the seawater, they get harder.

- **Like a chicken's egg**, a shark egg contains a yolk that feeds the baby as it grows bigger.

- **Inside the egg**, a shark baby grows for between six and ten months before hatching.

- **You can sometimes find empty shark eggcases** washed up on beaches. They're known as 'mermaid's purses'.

◀ *A fully formed Port Jackson shark emerges from its spiral-shaped egg case.*

Shark young

- **Not all sharks lay eggs.** Some give birth to live young instead. They're called 'viviparous' or 'ovoviviparous' sharks.

- **In ovoviviparous sharks**, such as basking sharks, the young grow inside eggs, but hatch while they are still inside the mother's body, before being born.

- **In viviparous sharks**, such as hammerheads, there are no eggs. The babies grow inside the mother's body from the start.

- **Young sharks** are called pups.

- **When a shark pup is born alive**, it usually slips out of its mother's body tail-first.

- **Most shark pups** look like smaller versions of their parents, but with a narrower body shape and stronger colours.

  ▶ Tiger shark pups are usually born at the end of spring or the beginning of summer. There can be between 10 and 80 pups in a litter.

- **Some species**, such as sand tiger sharks, have just two pups in a litter.

- **Whale sharks** are thought to be able to give birth to up to 300 pups at a time.

- **Shark parents** don't look after their babies. Once a pup is born, or hatches from its egg, it has to look after itself.

- **In sand tiger sharks** and several other species, the biggest, strongest pups eat the others while they are still inside their mother's body.

Growing up

- **Sharks grow slowly.** It can take a pup up to 20 years to grow into an adult.

- **Blue sharks are among the fastest growers.** A blue shark pup grows about 30 cm longer every year.

- **As shark pups are small**, predators often try to eat them. The biggest danger comes from other adult sharks. Sometimes, pups even get eaten by adults of their own species.

- **For every ten shark pups born,** only one or two will survive to be adults.

- **Many types of shark pups** live in 'nursery areas' – shallow parts of the sea close to the shore, where there are plenty of hiding places to shelter in and smaller sea creatures to feed on.

- **Sharks are born** with a full set of teeth, so they can start hunting for their own food straight away. Unlike the young of birds, humans, dogs and cats, shark pups are never fed by their parents.

- **Young sharks eat things** such as small fish, shrimps and baby octopuses.

- **A typical shark** lives for around 25 to 30 years, although some species, such as whale sharks and dogfish sharks, may live for 100 years or more.

- **When a shark dies**, scientists are able to tell how old it is by counting growth rings in its spine – like the rings inside tree trunks.

- Even when they reach adulthood, sharks don't stop growing. They just grow more slowly.

  ◀ As a baby shark grows, it feeds on the yolk from its egg. This is a lanternshark pup with its yolk.

Shark companions

- **There are several types of sea creatures** that like to hang around sharks. They include some fish species, and many parasites that feed on a shark's skin, blood or insides.

- **Small crablike creatures** called copepods attach themselves to a shark's eyes, gills, snout or fins. They nibble the shark's skin or suck its blood.

- **Sea leeches** bite sharks on their undersides and suck their blood.

- **Barnacles** are tiny sea creatures with shells. They fix themselves to rocks, boats, and large animals such as whales and sharks.

- **Whale sharks** sometimes try to get rid of skin parasites by rubbing themselves against boats.

- **Inside their bodies**, many sharks have parasites such as tapeworms. They live in a shark's gut and feed on its food.

- **Pilot fish** swim alongside sharks to hitch a ride on the shark's slipstream – the currents it makes in the water.

- **Sometimes a shark** and another species can help each other. This kind of relationship between two animals is called 'symbiosis'.

- **Remoras or 'shark suckers'** are fish that attach themselves to sharks using suction pads on their heads. They hitch a ride on the shark's body and feed on scraps of food left over by the shark.

> ★ STAR FACT ★
> Sharks open their mouths to let tiny cleaner wrasse fish nibble lice and dead skin from between their teeth. As the wrasse are helping the sharks, they don't get eaten.

▼ *A silvertip shark with a much smaller fish swimming along in its slipstream.*

Where sharks live

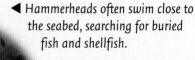

- **Sharks are found** in seas and oceans all around the world.

- **Sharks are almost all marine fish** – which means they live in the salty sea rather than in fresh water.

- **Just a few shark species** such as bull sharks and Ganges sharks can survive in fresh water, and swim out of the sea into rivers and lakes.

- **Sharks are most common around coasts**. Many species like to live in shallow sandy bays, near coral reefs, or in the medium-deep water a few miles from the shore.

◀ Hammerheads often swim close to the seabed, searching for buried fish and shellfish.

- **Coral reefs and seaweed forests** are a good home for young sharks. They provide them with food and shelter.

- **Sharks that live out in the open ocean**, such as blue sharks, are known as pelagic sharks.

- **Many types of sharks** spend most of their time on the ocean floor. They're called benthic sharks.

- **Many sharks like warm waters**, but a few, such as the Greenland shark, live in cold water around the Arctic.

- **Sharks are hardly ever found** in the Southern Ocean around Antarctica – probably because it's too cold for them there.

> ★ STAR FACT ★
> Epaulette sharks are often found in rock pools. They can move from one pool to another across dry land, by dragging themselves with their strong pectoral fins.

Sharks at home

- **Most sharks** don't have a fixed home. They swim anywhere they like, looking for food or a mate.

- **Sharks don't build nests**, dig burrows, or make any other kind of shelter.

- **A territory** is an area that a wild animal marks out for itself and guards against rivals.

- **Many animals are territorial**, but scientists are still trying to find out how territorial sharks are.

- **Some shark species** seem to have a territory that they patrol and guard.

- **White-tip reef sharks** stay in the same area for several months or years, although they don't defend it like a true territory.

- **Some sharks**, such as horn sharks, pick a special nursery area to lay their eggs in.

> ★ STAR FACT ★
> The Portuguese shark has been found in depths of 2640 m – deeper than any other shark.

- **Some shark species**, such as nurse sharks, use underwater sea caves as a place to rest during the day.

- **Some sharks have special preferences** about where they live. The Galapagos shark is only found around groups of small oceanic islands.

▶ A nurse shark rests quietly in a cave in a coral reef. Many sharks use caves as hiding places.

Long-distance travel

- **Many types of sharks** travel long distances in the course of their lives.

- **As all the world's seas and oceans** are connected, it's easy for sharks to cover huge distances.

- **Dogfish sharks** that have been tagged and released back into the sea can be located over 8000 km away from where they were first caught.

- **Migrating** means moving around, usually from season to season, according to a regular pattern.

- **The longest migrations** are made by blue sharks. They follow the Gulf Stream current across the Atlantic from the Caribbean Sea to Europe, then swim south along the African coast, then cross the Atlantic again to return to the Caribbean.

- **Blue sharks** can cover over 6000 km in one year.

- **Sharks sometimes migrate** in order to mate in one part of the sea, then move far away to another area to lay their eggs somewhere safer.

- **Another reason for sharks to migrate** is to follow shoals of fish as they move around the oceans, in order to feed on them.

- **Scientists think sharks** may use their ampullae of Lorenzini to detect the Earth's magnetic field, helping them to navigate over long distances.

- **Many sharks**, like spined pygmy sharks, spend the daytime in deep water, but swim up to the surface at night. This is called vertical migration.

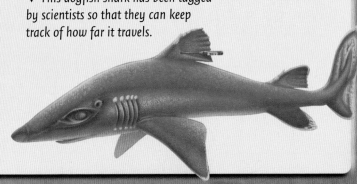

▼ *This dogfish shark has been tagged by scientists so that they can keep track of how far it travels.*

Types of shark

- **Scientists divide the 400 species** of sharks into eight large groups, called orders, and around 30 smaller groups, or families.

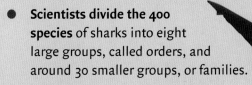

- **Arranging sharks into groups,** or 'classifying' them, helps scientists to study them and identify them.

- **Scientists often disagree** about how to classify sharks, so there are several different ways to do it.

- **Shark orders and families** have long scientific names. For example, goblin sharks belong to the Mitsukurinidae family, in the order Lamniformes.

- **Some shark groups** have common names too. The Lamniformes, for example, are also known as mackerel sharks.

- **Each shark species** has its own scientific name, which is written in Latin. For example, the great white shark is *Carcharodon carcharias*.

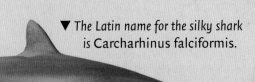

▼ *The Latin name for the silky shark is Carcharhinus falciformis.*

- **Scientists decide** which group a shark belongs to by looking at things like its body shape, markings and behaviour.

- **Sometimes,** very different-looking sharks can belong to the same group. Huge whale sharks and small, slender epaulette sharks are both in the same order.

- **Some sharks** have several different names. For example, the sand tiger shark is also known as the sand shark, the ragged-tooth shark, or the grey nurse shark.

- **There may still be unknown types of sharks** that scientists have not yet discovered.

Great white sharks

- **The great white** is the most famous of all sharks.
- **Belonging to the mackerel shark group**, great white sharks are fast, fierce hunters.
- **A typical great white shark** is around 4 to 5 m long – slightly longer than a car.
- **The biggest great whites** on record were over 7 m long.

> ★ STAR FACT ★
> Scientists do not know exactly how great whites reproduce, where they migrate to or how long they live.

- **Great white sharks** are often found in medium-warm waters such as those around Australia and Japan.
- **They sometimes attack humans**, but great whites much prefers to eat fish, seals and sealions.
- **Great white sharks are not white all over**. They are grey on top, with a pale grey or creamy underside.
- **When swimming**, great whites will sometimes stick their heads out of the water, or leap high into the air.
- **It is difficult** to keep a great white in captivity. If they are put into an aquarium, they only live for a few days.

◄ *Great whites have massive, powerful jaws and huge teeth, ideal for ripping viciously into their prey.*

Mako sharks

◄ *The shortfin mako is the faster of the two species of mako shark.*

- **There are two species of mako** – the shortfin and the longfin. The longfin has longer pectoral fins.
- **The name 'mako'** comes from the Maori name for the shark, mako-mako – which means 'man-eater'. Makos are common around New Zealand, the home of the Maori people. They are also found in oceans all around the world.
- **Swift and fierce makos** are strong, muscular hunting sharks that can swim at great speed.
- **Makos are closely related** to great white sharks and live and hunt in a similar way. They will sometimes attack humans but they usually eat fish.
- **Makos have long, graceful bodies** and pointed snouts.
- **Makos are known for their vivid colours**. They are dark purplish-blue on top and silvery-white underneath.
- **Makos grow** up to 4 m long.
- **Mako sharks' teeth** are very narrow and pointed to help them grab slippery fish in their jaws.
- **People often fish for makos** as a sport and they are also caught to use as food.
- **Makos are also known as** bonito sharks or blue pointers.

Thresher sharks

- **There are three species of thresher** – the common, the pelagic, and the bigeye thresher.

- **Thresher sharks** are easily recognized by their extremely long tails. The upper lobe, or part, of a thresher's tail can be up to 50 percent of the shark's whole body length

- **Including the tail**, threshers can grow up to 6 m long.

- **Threshers use their amazing tails** to round up shoals of small fish such as sardines or herrings. Then they stun the fish by beating (or 'threshing') them with their tails, before eating them.

- **Although threshers are big**, their mouths are small so they only eat small prey.

- **Threshers hardly ever attack humans**. But they have been known to injure fishermen by hitting them with their tails.

▼ Thresher sharks use their enormous tails by sweeping them from side to side. Because the tail is so long, its sweeping or 'threshing' movements can hit dozens of fish at once.

★ STAR FACT ★
Thresher sharks have a reputation for being very cunning. Because of this, the ancient Greeks and Romans called them 'fox sharks'.

- **Common threshers** are the best-known and are often seen near the shore.

- **Pelagic threshers** get their name because they prefer to stay in the pelagic zone – the open sea, away from the shore.

- **Bigeye threshers** often live deep down in the sea. Their eyes are up to 10 cm across.

The thresher's teeth are small and triangle-shaped, but they are very sharp

The thresher's tail can be up to 3 m long

Sandtiger sharks

- **A typical sand tiger shark** is around 3.2 m long.

- **Sand tiger sharks** are not closely related to tiger sharks. They belong to a different order, and are more closely related to makos and great whites.

- **Sand tiger sharks don't have stripes** – they have brownish spots instead.

- **They are called sand tiger sharks** because they swim over the sandy seabed, and because of their large teeth.

- **Sharks often circle their prey** before closing in for the kill.

- **Sandtiger sharks are not very dangerous** to humans.

- **The diet of sand tiger sharks** is mainly fish and sometimes they kill and eat bigger animals such as sealions.

> ★ STAR FACT ★
> Sand tiger sharks have been known to approach divers who are spear-fishing, and grab the fish off their spears.

- **When hunting**, sand tiger sharks sometimes work in groups, surrounding a shoal of fish and feeding on them together, in a 'feeding frenzy'.

- **Sand tigers are popular in aquariums**, as they look exciting and survive well in captivity.

◀ Sandtiger sharks can hold air in their stomachs so they can stay afloat without moving.

Porbeagle sharks

- **To help porbeagle sharks swim faster** they have a second keel (ridge) on their tails.

- **Like great white sharks**, porbeagles are grey on top and white underneath. Porbeagles also have a white mark on the dorsal fin.

- **Porbeagle sharks** grow up to 3 m long.

- **Cooler seas** are the preferred habitat of porbeagle sharks.

- **Porbeagles can make their bodies warmer** than their surroundings. This helps them to stay warm in their chilly habitat.

▶ A porbeagle shark chasing mackerel, its favourite food.

- **Porbeagle sharks used to be known as** mackerel sharks.

- **The diet of porbeagles** is mostly fish and squid. They will chase shoals of mackerel long distances.

- **Porbeagles are aggressive** and can attack people. However, these are very rare, because people don't usually swim in cold water.

- **Porbeagle sharks are among the few fish** that are known to play. They will roll over and over at the sea surface and wrap themselves in seaweed.

- **The name 'porbeagle'** is thought to be a combination of porpoise (which the porbeagle resembles) and beagle, a dog known for its determination and toughness.

Basking sharks

- **Unlike its cousins**, great whites and makos, the basking shark is a gentle giant.

- **The basking shark** is the second-biggest shark in the world, after the whale shark. It grows up to 9 m long – as long as five people lying end-to-end.

- **Basking sharks are filter-feeders**, and eat by sieving tiny animals, known as plankton, out of the water as they swim along.

- **Basking sharks are not interested** in eating humans – as they don't have big teeth for biting or chewing.

- **Basking sharks get their name** because they appear to 'bask', or lie in the sun, close to the surface of the sea. When they do this they are probably feeding.

◀ Krill are like tiny prawns. They are just one of the many small sea animals that make up the basking shark's diet of plankton.

- **Basking sharks will sometimes leap** right out of the water, and then flop back down with an enormous splash.

- **Other names for basking sharks** are bone sharks, elephant sharks, bigmouth sharks, or sunfish – because people used to think basking sharks enjoyed lying in the sun.

- **Occasionally** basking sharks have been seen swimming in large groups of 50 or more.

- **People used to catch basking sharks** and collect the oil from their livers to use as lamp fuel. Because basking sharks are so big, one basking shark liver could provide a huge amount of lamp oil.

> ★ STAR FACT ★
> Basking sharks have huge livers that
> weigh up to 2000 kg.

Goblin sharks

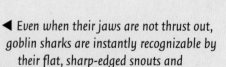

- **With incredibly long, flattened, pointed snouts**, goblin sharks look very strange. They can stick their jaws right out of their heads.

- **The goblin shark's long snout** looks like a weapon – but in fact scientists think it helps the shark find prey using its sense of electrical detection.

- **Goblin sharks** have pale pink skin which is much softer and flabbier than the skin of most sharks.

- **When its jaws are not pushed forward**, the goblin shark looks fairly similar to other sharks.

- **When it is about to catch prey**, a goblin shark thrusts its jaws out so far they look like a second snout.

- **Goblin sharks feed on fish**, squid and crustaceans such as crabs and lobsters.

◀ Even when their jaws are not thrust out, goblin sharks are instantly recognizable by their flat, sharp-edged snouts and bubblegum-pink colour.

- **A goblin shark has sharp teeth** at the front of its mouth for grabbing prey and smaller teeth at the back of its mouth for chewing.

- **Most goblin sharks** are between 1 m to 2 m long.

- **As goblin sharks are rarely caught** scientists still don't know much about them.

> ★ STAR FACT ★
> Goblin sharks probably got their name
> because of their strange appearance –
> although they don't really look like goblins!

Crocodile sharks

- **Scientists** are still trying to find out more about the little-known crocodile shark.

- **When fully grown** crocodile sharks are quite small – around 1 m long.

- **The crocodile shark** has huge eyes compared to its body size. They take up almost half its head.

- **Female crocodile sharks** always give birth to four babies at a time.

- **Small fish**, squid and shrimps are the main diet of the crocodile shark.

- **Humans have only known about** crocodile sharks since 1936, when one was discovered in a fish market in Japan.

> ★ STAR FACT ★
> Crocodile sharks cause problems for humans by biting through undersea communications cables.

- **The crocodile shark's name** comes from its Japanese name, mizuwani, meaning 'water crocodile'. It is so named because it has pointed teeth and snaps its jaws like a crocodile.

- **Crocodile sharks don't attack people**, but if caught they often bite fishermen on the hand.

- **One of the crocodile shark's closest relatives** is the megamouth shark – even though they're very different in size and feeding habits.

◀ *Its big teeth and large eyes make it look threatening, but the crocodile shark is no bigger than an average-sized dog.*

Megamouth sharks

- **One of the most recently** discovered sharks is the megamouth. It is probably one of the rarest sharks.

- **The first known megamouth** was caught in 1976, off the islands of Hawaii.

- **The megamouth grows** to over 5 m long. It has a very thick, rounded, heavy body and a huge head.

- **Megamouth sharks are filter-feeders**. They feed at night, cruising along near the ocean surface with their mouths wide open to filter plankton out of the water.

▶ *It's easy to see how the megamouth got its name. Its mouth is so big, an armchair could fit inside it.*

> ★ STAR FACT ★
> Less than 20 megamouth sharks have ever been found.

- **During the day**, a megamouth swims down to depths of 200 m or deeper.

- **The megamouth** gets its name because its mouth is so big – up to 1.3 m wide.

- **The scientific name** of the megamouth is *Megachasma pelagios*, which means 'huge yawner of the open sea'.

- **The mouth** of the megamouth shark is right at the front of its snout, not underneath as in most sharks.

- **Megamouths have been caught** around the world in the Pacific, Atlantic and Indian Oceans.

Tiger sharks

▼ A fierce tiger shark closes in on a seal, ready to make a meal of it. Some tiger sharks can rival great whites in size.

The tiger shark is very large and powerful, and could swallow this monk seal in one gulp

Like many other sharks, the tiger shark thrusts its teeth forward to bite

- **One of the most dangerous sharks in the sea** is the tiger shark. It will attack almost anything, including humans.

- **Tiger sharks are usually** about 3 m long, but they can grow to 6 m.

- **Young tiger sharks** have stripes to camouflage them and protect them from predators. As a tiger shark gets older, its stripes fade.

- **Tiger sharks have massive heads** with a blunt snout, large eyes and a wide mouth.

- **The diet of tiger sharks** consists of fish, seals, sealions, turtles, shellfish, crabs, seabirds, dolphins, crocodiles, squid and jellyfish. They also take bites out of bigger animals such as whales.

- **Tiger sharks have even been seen** eating other tiger sharks.

- **Many unusual objects**, such as oil drums, tin cans, glass bottles, clothes, rubber tyres, coal, cushions and tools, and even pieces of armour have been found in the stomachs of tiger sharks.

- **The tiger shark** is found in most of the world's warmer seas and oceans.

- **Tiger sharks sometimes swim** into the mouths of rivers.

> ★ STAR FACT ★
> Tiger sharks might eat metal objects because they give off a slight electrical signal, which the shark can detect with its electrical sense. It probably mistakes them for living things.

Bull sharks

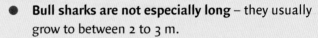

- **Bull sharks** are powerful, ferocious and aggressive hunting sharks.

- **The bull shark gets its name** because its body is thick, stocky and muscular, like a bull.

- **Like the tiger shark**, the bull shark belongs to a family of sharks called requiem sharks.

- **Requiem sharks** probably got their name because of the French word for shark, *requin*.

- **Bull sharks are not especially long** – they usually grow to between 2 to 3 m.

- **Bull sharks are among the few sharks** that can survive in fresh water. They swim hundreds of kilometres up rivers such as the Mississippi, the Amazon and the Zambezi.

- **One group of bull sharks** lives in Lake Nicaragua, a huge lake in Central America.

- **Bull sharks are often known by other names**, depending on where they live – such as the Zambezi river shark or the Nicaragua shark.

- **The bull shark is very dangerous**, and often lurks in shallow water where humans swim.

- **Bull sharks have attacked humans so often**, some experts think they may be the most dangerous sharks of all.

◀ A bull shark swims along in shallow water with a remora fish below it.

Blue sharks

- **One of the fastest sharks** in the sea, blue sharks can reach a top speed of almost 30 km/h.

- **Sleek, slim and graceful,** the body of the blue shark is around 4 m long.

- **The blue shark really is blue**. It's a deep, silvery indigo on top, with a paler underside.

- **The migration route** of the blue shark is notoriously long. They travel right across oceans, making trips of 3000 km or more.

- **A blue shark can travel** more than 60 km in a day.

- **The blue shark was once** one of the most common sharks, and they are found in almost every part of every ocean. Its population is now falling fast because so many have been caught by humans.

◀ Blue sharks have very slender, flexible bodies, with long snouts and long, narrow fins.

- **Blue sharks are fished for food**, but many more are caught by accident by hooks or nets meant for tuna and swordfish.

- **Experts have estimated** that 6 million blue sharks are caught and killed every year.

- **Blue sharks eat mostly squid**, although they will try any kind of fish or other sea creature.

> ★ STAR FACT ★
> Blue sharks don't normally attack people, but they have been reported to go into feeding frenzies to attack the survivors of sunken ships.

White-tip sharks

- **There are two quite different sharks** that have the name 'white-tip' – the white-tip reef shark and the oceanic white-tip shark.

- **The white-tip reef shark** is a common shark about 1.5 m long.

- **Distinctive white tips** on their tails and dorsal fins make white-tip reef sharks easily recognizable.

- **Swimmers and divers** often spot white-tip reef sharks because they inhabit in coral reefs, sea caves and shallow water during the day.

- **Warm seas** such as the Persian Gulf and the waters around Australia and the Pacific islands are home to many white-tip reef sharks.

- **White-tip reef sharks go hunting** at night for squid and octopus.

- **White-tip reef sharks rarely bother people**, except to steal fish from fishing spears.

- **The oceanic white-tip shark** is a large, fast hunting shark, around 3 m long. It lives in the open oceans.

- **The oceanic white-tip shark sometimes**, but not always, has a white or pale grey mark on its dorsal fin.

- **Oceanic white-tips can be dangerous**. They are attracted to shipwrecks and plane wrecks in the sea, and may attack the survivors.

▶ A white-tip reef shark in its favourite habitat, a shallow coral reef. The white tips on its fins and tail make it easy to identify.

Black-tip sharks

- **A medium-sized shark**, the black-tip reef shark is around 1.5 m long.

- **Like its cousin** the white-tip, the black-tip reef shark likes warm, shallow water.

- **Black-tip reef sharks** have black marks on the tips of all their fins.

- **Black-tips are sometimes** known as 'black sharks'.

- **The black-tip reef shark** has long, slender teeth ideally suited to snapping up its main prey – fish that live around coral reefs.

- **Scuba divers** often encounter black-tip reef sharks, but they're rarely aggressive – although they have been known to bite people's legs and feet.

- **Another shark, the spinner shark**, is also known as the black-tip shark. It's a completely different species from the black-tip reef shark, and grows to about 2 m long.

- **The black-tip or spinner shark** also has black tips on all its fins.

- **Spinner sharks get their name** because they sometimes leap out of the water and spin around in the air.

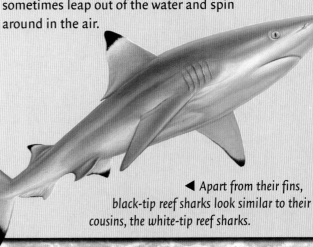

★ STAR FACT ★
Since the Suez Canal was built, black-tip reef sharks have swum through it from the Red Sea, and now live in the Mediterranean Sea too.

◀ Apart from their fins, black-tip reef sharks look similar to their cousins, the white-tip reef sharks.

Bonnethead sharks

- **Bonnetheads** are a type of hammerhead shark.

- **This shark's head** looks less like a hammer, and more like a rounded bonnet or shovel shape.

- **Bonnetheads** are the smallest hammerheads, averaging around 1 m long.

- **Bonnetheads form huge groups** – sometimes there can be thousands of them in a school.

- **The bonnethead shark** is often found in shallow bays and river estuaries. They mainly eat crabs, shrimps and other crustaceans.

- **Scientists think bonnetheads** have complex social systems, with different members of a group having different levels of importance.

- **Bonnetheads are also called bonnet sharks,** bonnetnose sharks, or shovelheads.

- **Fishermen have to be careful** if they grab a bonnethead by the tail, as it can reach up and bite their hand.

- **The scalloped bonnethead** is another type of hammerhead shark. Its bonnet-shaped head has curved or scallop-shaped lines on it.

◀ A bonnethead shark swallows a ray it has just found part-buried in the sand.

★ STAR FACT ★
Dominant bonnethead sharks keep other individuals in their place with behaviour such as head-shaking, jaw-snapping and butting.

Hammerhead sharks

- **Hammerhead sharks** are probably the strangest-looking sharks of all. Their heads really do look like the ends of hammers.

- **A hammerhead's head** is extremely wide. The shark's eyes are at either end of the 'hammer', making them a very long way apart.

- **Experts think hammerheads' heads** may help them to find food by spreading out their ampullae of Lorenzini (electrical detectors) over a wide area.

- **Seen from the side**, a hammerhead looks similar to a normal shark, as the 'hammer' is so flat and streamlined.

- **There are nine species of hammerhead**. They include great, scalloped, smooth, wingheads and bonnethead sharks.

◄ A hammerhead shark's head is a wide, flat, oblong shape that looks like a hammer when seen from above.

- **The great hammerhead** is the biggest. It can reach 6 m long and has been known to attack humans.

- **Hammerheads go hunting alone** at night for fish, squid, octopuses, crabs and stingrays.

- **By day**, hammerheads often swim in large groups.

- **Hammerheads have unusually long dorsal fins**. They are often seen swimming with their dorsal fins sticking out of the water.

- **The winghead shark has the widest head** of any shark. It can measure as much as half the shark's body length.

Lemon sharks

★ STAR FACT ★
When a male and female lemon shark meet up to mate, they swim along side by side, so closely that they can look like a two-headed shark.

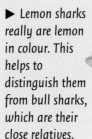

► Lemon sharks really are lemon in colour. This helps to distinguish them from bull sharks, which are their close relatives.

- **The lemon shark** gets its name from its yellowish colour, especially on the underside.

- **Lemon sharks are fish-eating sharks** related to tiger and bull sharks.

- **Lemon sharks grow** up to 3 m long.

- **People sometimes confuse** lemon sharks with bull sharks, as they have a similar shape.

- **Apart from the colour**, you can tell a lemon shark because its two dorsal fins are almost the same size (in most sharks, the first dorsal fin is much bigger).

- **Lemon sharks survive** very well in captivity and might be seen in an aquarium or sealife centre.

- **Since lemon sharks can be kept in tanks**, scientists often use them for experiments.

- **When lemon sharks are young**, they eat small fish, sea worms and shrimps. As they get older, they feed on seabirds, rays and lobsters.

- **Lemon sharks have been found with stings** from stingrays embedded in their mouths.

Houndsharks

- **There are over 30** different species of houndsharks.

- **Houndsharks** are a family of smallish sharks around 1.5 m long.

- **Most types of houndsharks** live on shallow seabeds, feeding on shellfish, crabs and lobsters.

- **Most houndsharks have flat teeth** used for crushing their prey.

- **Houndsharks** belong to a different shark order to dogfish and dog sharks.

- **Whiskery sharks** are a type of houndshark with barbels – finger-like organs on their snouts that look like whiskers. They help the shark feel its way along the seabed

- **The tope shark** is a houndshark with a pointy snout. It's also called the vitamin shark because it used to be hunted for its liver oil that was used as a health food.

◄ *The leopard shark is one of the most distinctive of all sharks. They are between 1 to 2 m long.*

- **The leopard shark** is an unmistakable species of houndshark. It gets its name from the beautiful leopard-like spots on its back.

- **Soupfin sharks** are houndsharks too. They get their name because their fins are used to make shark's fin soup – although other sharks are used for this too.

- **Gummy sharks** are another type of houndshark – named because they seem to have have no teeth. Like other houndsharks, they simply have flat, grinding teeth instead of sharp ones.

Weasel sharks and catsharks

- **You can spot a weasel shark** because it looks as if it's had a bite taken out of its tail. This is actually a natural dent in the tail called the 'precaudal pit'.

- **Weasel sharks are a type of small shark** just over 1 m long.

- **There are several different species of weasel sharks**, including the hooktooth, the sickelfin weasel and the snaggletooth.

- **Catsharks** are a separate shark family from weasel sharks. There are over 40 catshark species.

- **Catsharks are less than 1 m in length** and eat small fish and crabs.

- **Catsharks get their name** because their eyes look like a cat's.

- **The lollipop catshark** is an unusual catshark with a very large head.

- **Many catsharks have beautiful markings.** The draughtboard shark, for example, is a catshark with dark and light checkerboard markings, while the chain shark has skin patterns that look like silver chains.

- **Shy-eye sharks** and swell sharks are both types of catsharks.

- **The false catshark** is not a catshark at all. At 3 m long, it's much bigger than a real catshark, and was given its name by mistake.

◄ *Weasel sharks are related to bull and lemon sharks, and have a typical shark shape.*

Dogfish sharks

- **Some of the most common sharks** are dogfish sharks. They include the piked and the spiny dogfish.

- **There is a huge family** of dogfish sharks, containing around 80 different species.

- **Dogfish sharks usually have spines** in front of their dorsal fins and they have no anal fin at all.

- **Dogfish sharks range in size** from less than 20 cm long to over 6 m long.

- **Millions of dogfish sharks** are caught every year – for their meat but also for their fins, oil and skin.

- **Spiny dogfish sharks are ground up** to be made into garden fertilizer.

> ★ STAR FACT ★
> In America, spiny dogfish used to be caught, dried and burnt as a fuel.

- **Spiny dogfish often cause problems** for fishermen. They tear up fishing nets and eat the fish and steal lobsters from lobster pots.

- **Many species of dogfish sharks** swim together in groups.

- **Dogfish sharks** may have got their name because they form packs, like dogs. In the past, any common type of plant or animal used to be given the name 'dog' – like the dog rose, for example.

◀ A group of dogfish sharks on the prowl. They sometimes form schools of hundreds or even thousands of individuals.

Greenland sharks

> ★ STAR FACT ★
> A reindeer was once found inside a dead Greenland shark's stomach.

- **The biggest type of dogfish shark** is the Greenland shark. It grows up to 6.5 m in length.

- **Greenland sharks** like cold water. They live in the north Atlantic, around Greenland, Iceland and Canada, and can stand temperatures as low as 2°C.

- **Gurry shark and sleeper shark** are other names for the greenland shark.

- **The Greenland is known as** the sleeper shark because it is sluggish and swims very slowly.

- **Luminescent copepods** (tiny sea creatures) live in the eyes of the greenland shark. They make the shark's eyes glow in the dark, which may help it by luring prey towards it.

- **Greenland sharks eat fish**, squid, seals and sealions, as well as scavenging on the dead bodies of whales.

- **In summer**, greenland sharks swim up to the surface to find food, but they spend the rest of their time swimming at depths of 1500 m.

- **Inuit people** caught Greenland sharks on lines through iceholes. They used the skin to make boots and the teeth for knife blades.

- **Fresh Greenland shark meat** is poisonous, but can be eaten safely if it is boiled several times.

◀ Greenland sharks are unusual in choosing to live in the deep, icy waters of the arctic – most sharks prefer shallow, warm seas.

Dwarf and pygmy sharks

- **The smallest sharks in the world** are dwarf and pygmy sharks. The spined pygmy shark and the dwarf dogshark are both around 18 to 20 cm long.

- **The pygmy shark** or slime shark is around 25 cm long.

- **Sharks this small** are harmless to humans.

▶ *Working as a group, spined pygmy sharks can attack a fish much larger than themselves.*

- **The spined pygmy shark** lives as deep as 2000 m down during the day, but at night it swims up to hunt in shallower water about 200 m deep.

- **The dwarf dogshark** is also found at great depths – as deep as 1000 m.

- **Dwarf and pygmy sharks** all have luminous undersides.

- **Although dwarf and pygmy sharks are small**, they hunt just like many larger sharks, snapping up fish, shrimps and octopuses.

- **The spined pygmy shark** was first discovered in 1908, off the coast of Japan. We now know it lives all around the world. It is also called the cigar shark, because of its size, slim shape and dark colour.

- **Dwarf and pygmy sharks** are hard to keep in captivity, as they prefer very deep water.

Prickly and bramble sharks

- **Almost all sharks** have rough skin, but the skin of prickly and bramble sharks is really rough.

- **The bramble shark** is a deepwater shark that has large, thornlike spikes scattered unevenly all over its body.

- **A bramble shark's spikes** are made of extra-large, extra-sharp denticles.

- **Bramble sharks grow** to about 3 m long.

- **Although they are large**, bramble sharks are rarely seen. This is because they live in deep water and are quite shy.

▼ *A bramble shark has the prickliest, roughest skin of any shark. Its whole body is scattered with sharp, thorny spikes.*

- **The prickly shark** is a relative of the bramble shark. It looks similar, but has smaller prickles.

- **Prickly sharks grow** to around 4 m long.

- **Prickly dogfish** belong to a separate family. They have deep bodies, and very rough skin rather than long prickles.

- **Though their skin is tough and prickly**, prickly dogfish have strangely soft, spongy lips.

Cookie-cutter sharks

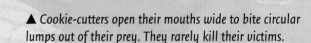
▲ Cookie-cutters open their mouths wide to bite circular lumps out of their prey. They rarely kill their victims.

- **Cookie-cutter sharks** are strange, deep water sharks that are found around the world.

- **There are two species**, the cookie-cutter and the large-tooth cookie-cutter.

- **The large-tooth cookie-cutter** is the smaller of the two, but it has bigger teeth. Its teeth are bigger in relation to its body size than those of any other shark.

- **Cookie-cutters belong** to the dogfish shark family.

- **Cookie-cutter sharks are brown** in colour, with greenish eyes.

- **Instead of eating whole animals**, cookie-cutters take bites out of much bigger sea creatures such as big sharks and whales.

- **To feed**, a cookie-cutter shark attaches itself to its prey by sucking with its mouth. Then it swivels its sharp teeth around in a circle until it has cut out a lump of flesh.

- **Cookie-cutters themselves are not big** – only around 50 cm long. Because they don't need to catch or kill their prey, they can feed on animals that are many times larger than they are.

- **Many sharks**, dolphins, porpoises and whales have permanent, round scars left by cookie-cutters.

► A close-up view of a cookie-cutter shark's unusual mouth and teeth.

> ★ **STAR FACT** ★
> Cookie-cutters have been known to take bites out of parts of submarines and undersea cables.

Carpet sharks

- **The carpet sharks** are a varied group of more than 30 different species of sharks.

- **Many carpet sharks** are less than 1 m long, but this group also includes the whale shark, the biggest shark of all.

- **Carpet sharks live** in warm tropical seas, like those around Australia, Indonesia and Arabia, and usually live in shallow waters around reefs and sandbars.

- **Carpet sharks like to lie still** on the seabed. Many of them have a slightly flattened body shape that helps them to camouflage themselves on the ocean floor.

- **Most carpet sharks** feed on seabed-dwelling prey such as crabs, shellfish, octopuses and sea worms.

- **Many carpet sharks** have beautiful speckled markings. They were named because these often resemble patterned carpets or tapestries.

- **Collared carpet sharks** can change colour to match their surroundings.

- **Epaulette sharks** are a type of carpet shark. They get their name because they have dark patches on their 'shoulders' – like epaulettes (cloth flaps) on a jacket.

- **Long-tailed carpet sharks** have extra-long tails, with long, fine fins that resemble fronds of seaweed.

- **The barbelthroat carpet shark** has barbels – fleshy finger shapes used for feeling things – on its throat. Only one example of this breed has ever been found.

▼ *The massive whale shark belongs to the carpet shark group. Its relatives include tiny carpet sharks such as the epaulette shark.*

Wobbegongs

- **Wobbegongs** belong to the carpet shark family.

- **The name 'wobbegong'** was given to these sharks by the Australian Aborigine people. Wobbegongs are often found in shallow, sandy water around the coast of Australia.

- **Wobbegongs can be quite large** – some, like the tasselled wobbegong, growing up to 4 m long.

- **Wobbegong have wide, flattened bodies** to help them hide on the seabed.

- **A typical wobbegong** has lots of barbels around its mouth.

- **The frilled wobbegong's barbels** are branched and frilly.

- **The tasselled wobbegong** has tassel-like barbels right around its face like a beard.

- **Wobbegong sharks**, also known as wobbies, feed on smaller fish and on other sea creatures such as crabs, octopuses and squid.

- **Wobbegongs have very strong jaws**, and can easily bite off a person's hand or foot.

- **Wobbegongs sometimes attack people** who accidentally step on them. For this reason, they have a reputation as being dangerous, although they are not interested in eating humans and rarely attack unless threatened.

◄ *A wobbegong shark lying in wait for prey on the seabed, disguised among seaweed and coral.*

Nurse sharks

- **The carpet shark group** includes nurse sharks, although unlike most carpet sharks they don't have carpet-like markings.

- Nurse sharks are usually brownish-grey, and sometimes have a few spots.

- **During the day**, nurse sharks often lie around on the seabed in groups.

- **At night**, nurse sharks wake up and go hunting.

- **Nurse sharks can reach** 4 m long, but most are nearer 3 m in length.

- **Nurse sharks have two barbels** hanging down underneath their noses. They use them to smell and feel their way along the seabed as they search for prey.

> ★ STAR FACT ★
> Divers sometimes grab nurse sharks' tails, hoping for a ride. The sharks don't like this and may turn around and bite.

- **Crabs, lobsters and sea urchins** are the preferred food of nurse sharks. They have flat, grinding teeth for crushing up shells.

- **If a nurse shark bites you**, it hangs on with a clamplike grip that's painful (though not deadly), and it can be almost impossible to dislodge them.

- **As they survive well in aquariums**, nurse sharks are often used in shark intelligence experiments.

◀ *A diver creeps close to a nurse shark hiding in a gap in a coral reef.*

Blind sharks

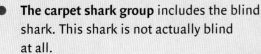

- **The carpet shark group** includes the blind shark. This shark is not actually blind at all.

- **When they are caught** and pulled out of the water, blind sharks close their eyes tightly and appear to have no eyes.

- **Blind sharks live** off the coast of Australia and are often found in shallow water near the shore. They hide in caves or crevices during the day and hunt at night.

- **There are two species of blind shark**. One is simply known as the blind shark, while the other is called Colclough's shark or the bluegray carpet shark.

- **The blind shark is yellow underneath** and brownish on top, with pale spots.

- ◀ *Blind sharks can see perfectly well in their natural habitat.*

- **At 1.3 m in length**, the blind shark is slightly bigger than Colclough's shark, which is just under 1 m long.

- **Young blind sharks** have dark stripes or bands across their bodies, which fade as they grow older.

- **Colclough's shark**, as its other name suggests, is blueish-grey in colour.

- **Both types of blind shark** feed by snuffling along the seabed for cuttlefish, shellfish and crabs.

- **Blind sharks have large spiracles**. These help them breathe even when their snouts are buried in the muddy seabed to find food.

Tawny and zebra sharks

- **Part of the carpet shark group**, tawny and zebra sharks are related to nurse, blind and whale sharks.

- **At 3 m in length**, the tawny shark is quite large. It lives in warm tropical seas close to the shore.

- **The tawny shark** is also known as the spitting shark because it spits out water as a defence if captured.

- **After spitting**, the tawny shark is said to grunt. It is one of the few sharks thought to make a noise.

- **The zebra shark** is another medium-sized carpet shark that grows up to 3 m long.

- **Distinctive dark and pale stripes** give zebra sharks their name – but they only have these when they are young. As they become adults, the stripes separate into blotches.

- **A zebra shark's egg cases** are a deep purplish-brown and have tufts of hair on them to help them lodge firmly among rocks and seaweed.

- **Like thresher sharks**, zebra sharks have very long tails.

- **Zebra sharks have long, hard ridges** running all the way down the backs and sides of their bodies. This helps divers to recognize them immediately.

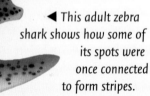

◄ This adult zebra shark shows how some of its spots were once connected to form stripes.

Whale sharks

- **The carpet shark group** also includes the whale shark.

- **Closest relatives of the whale shark** are wobbegongs and nurse sharks – not other filter-feeders like basking sharks and megamouths.

- **Whale sharks are the biggest sharks** in the world. Their average length is 10 to 12 m long – as long as a six or seven adult humans lying end-to-end.

- **The filter-feeding whale shark** sieves tiny plankton out of the water.

- **To feed**, whale sharks swim along with their massive mouths streched wide. A whale shark's mouth can be 1.5 m across.

- **A whale shark has around 3000 tiny teeth**, but it doesn't use them to eat with. Instead, it uses bristles in its gills to trap its food.

- **Whale sharks are covered** with pale stripes and spots.

▲ As a whale shark cruises along it sometimes swallows larger fish such as tuna, which can grow to 4 m long.

- **Scientists think** some whale sharks could live to be 100 years old or more.

- **Whale sharks might look dangerous**, but they're harmless to humans.

Hornsharks

- **The relatively small hornshark** has its own order, or shark group. It reaches 1.0 m to 1.5 m in length.

- **Hornsharks get their name** because they have poisonous spines, or horns, in front of both their dorsal fins.

- **Because of their large, rounded heads**, hornsharks are also called bullhead sharks.

- **Hornsharks have piglike snouts** and large lumps above their eyes that look like eyebrows.

◀ Hornsharks use the sharp spines near their fins to defend themselves against any predators that try to catch them.

- **Crabs and sea urchins** are the preferred food of hornsharks.

- **Hornsharks are only found** in the Pacific and Indian Oceans.

- **After laying**, the female hornshark takes each egg case in her mouth and jams it into a rock crevice to keep it safe. The eggcases are spiral-shaped.

- **Spines from hornsharks** are sometimes made into jewellery.

- **The Port Jackson shark** is a type of hornshark, named because it was discovered living in the bay of Port Jackson, Australia.

> ★ STAR FACT ★
> Some hornsharks have red-stained teeth because of all the sea urchins they eat.

Angel sharks

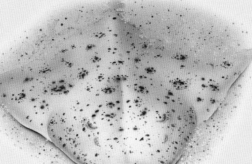
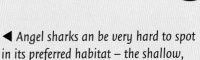

- **The angel shark order** contains about ten species of sharks. They get their name because of their wide, winglike fins.

- **Monkfish** is another name for angel sharks, because people used to think their fins looked like a monk's robes.

- **Another name for angel sharks** is sand devils, because they lie on the scabed and sometimes bite people who tread on them.

- **Angel sharks have very flattened bodies**. Most are around 1.5 m long.

- **The biggest angel shark** is the Japanese angel shark, which reaches 2 m long. It is hunted for food and was once also used to make shagreen (sharkskin sandpaper).

◀ Angel sharks an be very hard to spot in its preferred habitat – the shallow, sandy seabed.

- **By burying themselves on the sandy seabed**, angel sharks are hidden from passing fish and shellfish. They leap out to catch their prey with their small but sharp teeth.

- **An angel shark can lie in wait** for over a week until the right food comes past.

- **Like wobbegongs** and other bottom-dwelling sharks, angel sharks are camouflaged with spotted, speckled skin patterns.

- **In some countries**, angel sharks are served as a delicacy in expensive restaurants, where they are always called monkfish.

- **Angel sharks are viviparous** – they give birth to live babies. There are usually around ten pups in a litter.

Saw sharks

- **Part of an order of five species of shark**, saw sharks have flat heads and long, saw-shaped snouts.

- **A saw shark's snout is called a rostrum**. It is pointed and has teeth of various sizes, called rostral teeth, sticking out all the way around it.

- **At around 1 m in length**, saw sharks are relatively small.

- **For their size**, saw sharks' 'saws' are very long compared to other sharks' snouts. The snout of a longnose saw shark can make up half its total body length.

- **Saw sharks use their saws** for digging up prey such as shellfish from the seabed. Then they slash and jab at the prey before eating it.

- **The two long barbels** halfway along its snout help the saw shark feel its way along the seabed.

- **People sometimes eat saw sharks** in Japan and Australia.

- **Most saw sharks are grey**, but one species, the Japanese saw shark, is a muddy brown.

- **Saw sharks should not be confused** with sawfish, which are a type of ray.

▼ A saw shark hunting for food using its snout and sensitive barbels, which can feel, smell and taste its fishy prey.

Frilled sharks

- **The frilled shark** is the only species in its family.

- **A strange-looking shark**, the frilled shark has big, frilly gill slits – the first pair reach right around its head like a collar.

- **The long, thin body of the frilled shark** reaches up to 2 m in length.

- **Frilled sharks** only have one dorsal fin, instead of two as in most sharks. This fin is positioned far back towards the shark's tail.

- **Because of its snakelike appearance**, the frilled shark is sometimes mistaken for an eel or a sea snake.

- **Found in the cold, deep water of the Pacific** and Atlantic Oceans, frilled sharks feed on octopuses and squid.

◄ The frilled shark is an extremely rare shark species.

- **With three sharp points** on each tooth, frilled sharks have very unusual teeth. This is one of the features that is used to identify this rare shark.

- **Frilled sharks** have six gill slits on each side. Only a few sharks have more than five (including the frilled shark's relatives, six-gill and seven-gill sharks, and the six-gill saw shark).

- **Scientists have found** that after female frilled sharks mate, they are pregnant for as long as three years.

- **People used to think** that the frilled shark had been extinct for millions of years, as it was only known from ancient fossils. Living frilled sharks were first discovered in the late 19th century.

Shark relatives

- **Sharks are closely related** to two other groups of fish – the batoids and the chimaeras.

- **The batoids** include rays, skates and sawfish.

- **Batoids range from plate-sized skates** to giant manta rays more than 8 m across.

- **There are more than 500 species of batoids** – more than there are species of sharks.

- **Most batoids have wide, flat heads and bodies**, and long tapering tails. They look similar to some types of sharks, such as angel sharks.

- **Like some sharks**, batoids spend most of their time on the seabed.

- **Batoids feed on** bottom-dwelling sea creatures such as clams, shrimps and flatfish.

- **Because sharks are often difficult to catch** and keep in captivity, scientists often study batoids instead. They are so similar to sharks that they can provide clues to how sharks live.

- **Chimaeras** are a group of fish that are like sharks in some ways and more like bony fish in other ways.

- **Like sharks**, batoids and chimaeras have light, flexible skeletons made of cartilage, instead of having bones like other fish.

▼ An electric ray, a type of batoid, resting on the seabed. Its eyes are on the top of its body.

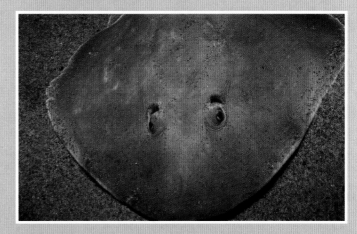

Rays

- **Close relatives of sharks**, rays are a type of batoid.

- **With their huge winglike fins**, some ray species wider than they are long.

- **A ray swims** using rippling motions of its fins and looks as if it is 'flying' along.

- **Many rays have a long, whiplike tail**. Unlike sharks, they don't use their tails to push themselves through the water.

- **Rays live in seas and oceans** all around the world, from shallows near the shore to seabeds 3000 m deep.

- **Rays have eyes on the tops of their heads** and large spiracles to breathe through. This enables them to see and breathe without difficulty, even while lying flat on the seabed.

- **Most rays are ovoviviparous** – they give birth to live young that have hatched from eggs inside their mothers' bodies.

- **Many rays are solitary** and like to live alone. However some, like golden cow-nosed rays, form huge groups of thousands of individuals.

- **Some rays**, such as the mangrove stingray and the huge manta ray, can leap right out of the water.

- **All rays are carnivores**. Some hunt for fish or shellfish, while others are filter-feeders.

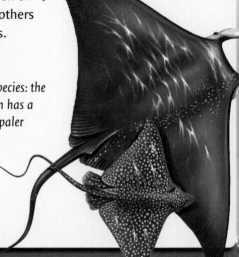

▶ Two different ray species: the huge manta ray, which has a dark upper side and a paler underside, and the smaller spotted eagle ray, which has a white underside and spots on top.

Types of rays

- **The biggest ray of all** is the manta ray. It is usually about 7 m wide by 7 m long (including the tail). The biggest are nearly 9 m wide.

- **The manta ray is a filter-feeder**, like the basking and whale sharks. It sucks in seawater and filters tiny plankton out of it.

- **Stingrays have a poisonous spine** (or sometimes two or three) in the middle of their tails. They are used mainly to defend themselves against attackers.

- **River stingrays**, unlike other rays, live in fresh water. They are found in rivers in Africa and South America, especially the river Amazon.

◀ Gill arches in the manta ray's mouth filter food from the water.

- **Round stingrays** have almost completely round, flat bodies, like dinner plates.

- **Electric rays can generate electricity** to give other animals a powerful electric shock. It can be used to put off predators, or to stun prey.

- **Short-nose electric rays** include some of the smallest rays, at less than 20 cm across.

- **The blind electric ray** is almost completely blind. It relies on its sense of electrical detection, which works like radar, to find prey.

- **Spotted eagle rays** are covered with beautiful pale spots on a dark background.

> ★ STAR FACT ★
> Stingray stings have often been used around the world to make pointed weapons.

Sawfish

▲ *A sawfish snout is the same width all the way along, with a gently curved tip.*

- **Another type of ray** is the sawfish.

- **Sawfish get their name** from their long, sawlike snouts, which are edged with sharp teeth like the teeth on a saw.

- **The green sawfish** grows to over 7 m long – longer than a great white shark.

- **The saw can account** for up to one-third of a sawfish's whole length.

- **Like rays**, sawfish have flattened bodies, but they look more like sharks than most rays do.

- **A sawfish uses its saw** to poke around for prey on the seabed and to slice into shoals of fish.

- **When young sawfish are born**, their snouts are soft and enclosed in a covering of skin. This protects the inside of the mother's body from being injured by the sharp teeth. After birth, the protective skin soon falls off and the saw becomes harder.

- **The large-tooth sawfish** sometimes swims up rivers in Australia.

- **Although sawfish look quite like saw sharks**, they are not the same at all. Sawfish are much bigger. They also have longer saws for their body size and no barbels.

> ★ **STAR FACT** ★
> Some sailors used to think sawfish sawed holes in boats in order to eat the passengers – but there is no evidence for this.

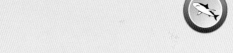

Skates

- **A relative of sharks**, skates are similar to rays, but they tend to have a straighter edges to the front of their pectoral fins and shorter tails.

- **Most types of skate** live in deep water, as far as 3000 m down.

- **Skates usually lie on the seabed** waiting for prey such as crabs and shrimps to come close.

- **As its mouth is on its underside**, the skate does not lunge at its prey. Instead it swim over it and grasps it from above.

◄ *The common skate can be recognized by its unusually long and pointed snout.*

- **Like some sharks**, skates lay eggs with protective cases around them.

- **Skate eggcases** have stiff spikes on them to help them stick into the seabed, and a sticky coating so that they soon become covered with sand or pebbles as a form of camouflage.

- **Skates are a very popular food** with people – especially the fins, which are called 'skate wings'.

- **The largest skates** include common and barndoor skates. They can reach 2 m to 3 m long (about the size of a large door).

- **The Texas skate** has two big spots, one on each wing. This may be a disguise that helps protect the skate by making it look like the eyes of a larger animal.

> ★ **STAR FACT** ★
> Sailors used to collect skates, dry them, twist them into strange shapes and sell them as miniature sea monsters.

Chimaeras

- **Although related to sharks**, chimaeras are not true sharks or rays. They belong to a separate group of cartilaginous fish.

- **Various types of chimaeras** are also known as ratfish, ghost sharks, spookfish and even 'ghouls'.

- **Chimaeras grow** to a maximum of around 2 m long, but most are small, from 60 cm to 100 cm long. Many chimaeras have very long tails, which can make up a large part of their body length.

- **Feeding on small fish** and octopuses, chimaeras usually live on the seabed.

- **Chimaeras are so called** because they look like a combination of different types of fish.

- **Like some sharks**, chimaeras have a spine in front of their dorsal fin.

▶ A ratfish (a type of chimaera) swimming close to the seabed. Chimaeras are found in the waters of the Arctic and the Antarctic.

★ STAR FACT ★
In Greek mythology, a chimaera was a monster that was part lion, part goat and part snake.

- **Another sharklike feature** of chimaeras is that they lay their eggs in eggcases. Chimaera eggcases are surprisingly large – some can be up to 40 cm long.

- **Like other fish**, Chimaeras have a covering over their gill slits. Sharks and rays do not have this.

- **Unlike sharks and rays**, chimaeras swim very slowly, and have fine, ribbed fins.

Sharks and humans

- **Sharks have been around** for much longer than humans have.

- **It's a natural instinct** for people to be scared of sharks, as some of them are fierce hunters.

- **However**, people are more dangerous to sharks than the other way around.

- **Some sharks**, such as Greenland sharks and angel sharks, are among the easiest fish to catch with a hook or fishing spear.

- **People hunt sharks** for all kinds of useful products such as sharkskin leather and liver oil.

- **People in the Pacific islands** used shark teeth to make tools and weapons as long as 5000 years ago.

★ STAR FACT ★
The word 'shark' is sometimes used to mean a ruthless person or a thief.

- **In the 5th century BC**, the ancient Greek historian Herodotus wrote about how sharks attacked sailors when ships sank during battles at sea.

- **The ancient Greek scientist Aristotle** studied sharks and was one of the first to notice that they were different from other fish.

- **Sharks are sometimes described** as vicious killers, but they only kill in order to survive.

◀ This photographer is using an underwater camera to get the best possible photo of a great white shark.

Fear of sharks

- **Many people** are very scared of being bitten or even eaten by a shark while swimming in the sea.

- **The great white shark** is the most feared shark.

- **Other large, fierce sharks** such as tiger and bull sharks also terrify people.

- **Although sharks can be dangerous**, our fear of them is out of proportion to how dangerous they are. Shark attacks are actually very rare.

- **One reason people find sharks so frightening** is that they live underwater, so it is hard to see them.

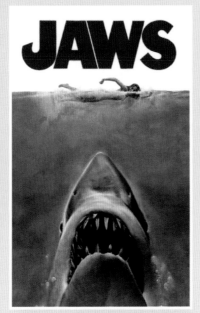

- **Another reason may be their big teeth and eyes** that seem to show no emotion. Humans instinctively prefer 'cute' animals to fierce-looking ones.

- **In the past**, sailors were famous for being superstitious. Their tales about sharks and shark attacks were probably exaggerated.

- **Fear of sharks** has been increased by the many books and films about shark attacks.

- **Shark attacks are rare**, so when they happen they are widely publicized. This makes sharks seem more dangerous than they really are.

◀ *A promotional poster for the film Jaws, about a killer great white shark. This poster exaggerates the shark by making it look much bigger than it really is.*

Shark attacks

- **There are less** than 100 reported cases worldwide every year of sharks attacking humans swimming or surfing in the sea.

- **Of these attacks**, fewer than 20 result in someone dying.

- **Most shark attacks** happen in shallow, water near the shore, because that's where sharks and swimmers are likely to be in the same place at the same time.

- **The worst shark tragedy ever** was in 1945, during World War II. A US warship was torpedoed and sank in the South Pacific, leaving 1000 crew members in the water. Before they could be rescued, over 600 of them had been eaten by sharks.

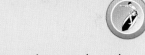

◀ *Sharks sometimes attack people surfing, maybe because, from below, a surfboard looks similar to a seal – a favourite food of the great white.*

- **In the summer of 1969**, four people were killed in shark attacks within two weeks off the coast of New Jersey, USA.

- **The areas with the most shark attacks** are the coasts of eastern North America, South Africa, and eastern Australia.

- **Sharks usually only attack** if they feel threatened, or if they mistake a human for prey, such as a seal.

- **Most shark attacks** happen in summer and during the afternoon.

- **Men are more likely** than women to be attacked by a shark, probably because more men go surfing and swim further out in the sea.

Survival stories

- **In 1749**, 14-year-old Brook Watson lost a leg to a shark while swimming at Havana, Cuba. He later became Mayor of London and was famous for his wooden leg.

- **Rodney Fox** was grabbed by a great white while taking part in a spear-fishing contest in Australia in 1963. His body was bitten right open, but he survived and went on to become a shark expert.

- **A great white shark** bit off undersea photographer Henri Bource's leg while he was diving off Australia in 1964. He was soon back at work in the same job, and four years later another shark bit his artificial leg!

- **In 1996**, surfer Joey Hanlon was attacked by a great white while surfing in California, USA. The shark bit into his torso, but he recovered after being given over 300 stitches.

- **Another surfer**, John Forse, was on his surfboard in Oregon, USA in 1998 when a great white shark grabbed his leg and pulled him deep underwater. He escaped by hitting the shark's dorsal fin until it let go.

> ★ STAR FACT ★
> In 2004, while snorkelling in Australia, Luke Tresoglavic was bitten by a small wobbegong that refused to let go. Tresoglavic had to swim to shore and drive to get help with the shark still attached to his leg.

- **13-year-old Bethany Hamilton** had her left arm bitten off by a tiger shark while surfing in Hawaii in 2003. She was surfing again within months.

- **Fishermen often get bitten** on the hands by sharks they have caught. Most of these shark bites are minor and go unreported.

- **Shark attack survivors** are often left with huge semicircular scars from the shark's teeth.

- **Today, shark attack victims** are more likely to survive than they used to be, thanks to fast boats and modern treatments such as blood transfusions.

▼ *Great whites are curious about unfamilar objects in the sea, and they will nearly always investigate because they are constantly on the lookout for food.*

Shark safety

- **Humans have developed** several ways to try to stay safe from shark attacks.

- **Swimming beaches** in shark areas are sometimes surrounded with strong nets to keep sharks out.

- **Chainmail diving suits** protect divers from sharks' teeth, but the body can still be crushed by a bite.

- **Some ships carry shark screens** – floating sacks that shipwreck survivors can climb inside. The screen disguises a person's shape and hides their scent, making them less likely to attract sharks.

- **Anti-shark weapons** can be used to scare sharks away. They include electrical prods that confuse a shark's electrical sense, and bangsticks, which are like underwater guns.

- **Some people have tried** to banish sharks by releasing chemicals they don't like the smell of into the water.

- **Some divers** wear striped diving suits for camouflage, so that it's harder for sharks to see them.

> ★ STAR FACT ★
> If you are ever attacked by a shark, you may be able to scare it off by punching its snout.

- **You shouldn't swim in a shark zone** if you have a cut or wound on your body. The blood could attract sharks.

- **If you see a large shark** when you're in the sea, the safest thing to do is to stay calm, avoid splashing about, and swim steadily towards the shore.

▲ *A great white shark showing how deadly its bite could be as it mouths the bars of an underwater shark-watching cage.*

Dangerous sharks

- **The great white shark** is often thought to be the most dangerous shark because it is most often identified in shark attacks. This is because it is easy to recognize. It is blamed for up to half of all serious shark attacks.

- **As well as biting humans**, great whites have been known to attack small boats.

- **Why are great whites so deadly?** It may be partly because they love eating seals and sealions, which look similar to humans in size and shape. The sharks simply get confused and attack the wrong prey.

- **Many experts think** bull sharks are actually more dangerous than great whites – but they are not well-known as killers because they are harder to identify.

- **After bull sharks attack**, they often escape unseen.

- **Not all dangerous sharks are fast hunters**. Nurse sharks and wobbegongs are usually placid and sluggish – but they can bite suddenly and hard if disturbed or annoyed.

- **Sharks with spines**, such as horn and dogfish sharks, are not deadly but often inflict painful injuries on people.

- **Stingrays**, which are related to sharks, can be killers – a few people die every year from their venom.

- **Sharks often bite** then swim away fast, making it hard to tell what species they are.

- **Huge basking sharks and manta rays**, though they don't bite, can be dangerous if they leap out of the water and land on a small boat.

Harmless sharks

- **The vast majority of shark species** are not interested in eating humans and never attack them.

- **Many sharks**, such as pygmy and zebra sharks, are so small they could not kill or eat a human even if they wanted to.

- **Most sharks can bite**, but will only do so if they themselves are attacked, caught or threatened.

- **Filter-feeders** such as whale sharks have very big mouths, but their throats are narrow, so they can't swallow a human.

- **Whale sharks** are often very friendly. They let snorkellers come close and even touch them.

- **Even big, dangerous sharks** such as the great white can get used to humans and become friendly enough to be stroked and tickled.

- **Harmless sharks** such as basking sharks are sometimes killed because they are mistaken for great whites or other dangerous sharks.

- **At some aquariums and sealife centres**, visitors can pay to climb into the tank with non-dangerous sharks.

- **Many shark scientists**, experts and photographers spend huge amounts of time with sharks without ever getting bitten.

- **Some people even keep small sharks** at home in fishtanks, although this is very difficult to do.

▼ *Although basking sharks are a massive 10 m in length, they are completely harmless.*

Shark fishing

- **Important species for fishing** include thresher sharks and various types of dogfish.

- **Most of the sharks** caught are used as food, though sharks have many other uses too.

- **Smaller sharks** such as the lesser spotted dogfish are caught by trawlers – boats that drag, or trawl huge fishing nets along behind them.

- **Flat, bottom-dwelling sharks** such as angel sharks can be caught by a diver using a fishing spear to stab through the shark onto the seabed.

- **Sea anglers go fishing** for sharks as a sport. Many coastal tourist resorts have special boats that take tourists sportfishing for sharks and other large fish. Sharks caught for sport are often thrown back alive.

▼ *Sharks are often caught in nets intended for fish such as tuna. Bycatch (unwanted catch) accounts for a significant proportion of shark fatalities.*

- **Sport fishermen** like to catch fast-swimming species, such as mako sharks, because they struggle a lot when they are hooked and so provide the most entertainment.

- **Whale sharks and other species** are sometimes hunted for their fins. After the fins are cut off, the rest of the shark is thrown back into the sea to die.

- **Millions of sharks** are caught by accident every year in nets meant for other sea creatures, such as squid.

- **Sharks are often caught** and killed just because there is a small risk that they might bite someone.

- **Humans catch** around 100 million sharks every year.

Sharks as food

- **Sharks are a nutritious food** because their flesh is very lean and full of protein. It often tastes good, too.

- **However, many people don't like the idea** of eating sharks, so when they are sold as food, sharks' names are often changed to things such as 'grayfish' or 'huss'.

- **In Japan** you can buy canned shark, smoked shark and shark fishcakes.

- **Raw shark** is eaten as part of traditional Japanese sashimi dishes.

- **Shark's-fin soup**, popular in Asia, is made by boiling shark fins to extract the gluey cartilage rods, which are the soup's main ingredient.

▶ *Shark liver oil has long been thought to have nutritional properties. Vitamin pills made from the oil are believed to help heal wounds and prevent flu.*

> ★ **STAR FACT** ★
> In Iceland, people eat dried, slightly rotted Greenland shark – a dish known as hakarl.

- **In the UK**, fish and chips is a popular takeaway meal. This fish is often a shark, the spiny dogfish – sold as 'rock salmon'.

- **Parts of sharks** are often made into health food supplements – such as shark liver oil tablets, which contain E and A vitamins. Some people even believe that eating shark can give you a shark's strength and courage, but there is no evidence for this.

- **Some types of Muslims** do not eat sharks as their religion forbids them to eat fish without scales.

- **Shark flesh goes off very fast**. It has to be eaten when fresh, or preserved by canning, smoking or pickling soon after being caught.

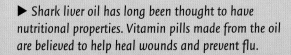

More uses for sharks

- **Polished shark skin leather** was once used to cover books and scientific objects such as telescopes.

- **Some species**, such as the spotted wobbegong, are still hunted for their skin. It's made into things such as shoes and handbags.

- **The ancient Greeks** used burnt angel shark skin to treat skin diseases, and shocks from electric rays as a painkiller during operations.

- **Squalene is an oil that is extracted from shark livers**. It is used in cosmetics, perfume, skin care and pharmaceutical products. It can take up to 3000 shark livers to produce one tonne of squalene.

- **Shark liver oil** is also used in some candles and paints.

- **Shark cartilage** is used to make a medicine for treating burns.

> ★ **STAR FACT** ★
> Shagreen – shark leather that still has its rough denticles – was used in the past to make non-slip grips for sword handles.

- **A type of medicine for heart disease** is made from chemicals extracted from sharks' blood.

- **Scientists have worked out** how to use shark corneas (the transparent protective covering in front of the eye) to make cornea transplants for humans.

- **Sharks' teeth** are often made into necklaces and other jewellery.

◀ *A handbag made from shark skin leather. Sharks that are hunted for their skin are usually species with beautiful mottled or speckled markings, such as the carpet shark.*

Shark tourism

- **People like to get close to sharks** because they are exciting and fiersome.

- **In coastal areas** around the world, tourists pay to see real sharks in their natural habitat.

- **Ecotourism** is tourism that helps preserve wild habitats and species. Some of the money paid by the ecotourists is used for conservation work.

- **Cage-diving** allows people to view dangerous sharks. They are lowered into the sea inside a metal cage.

- **People can view great whites** in Australia and South Africa.

- **People swim with sharks.** You can go on dives and snorkelling trips to see species such as reef and whale sharks.

- **On shark-feeding tours**, tourists go diving to the seabed, where a guide uses frozen fish to attract species such as white-tip reef sharks.

★ STAR FACT ★
Unlike dolphins and sealions, sharks don't perform for an audience. It's very hard to train a shark to learn complicated tricks.

- **Sharks attract visitors** to sealife centres and aquariums, where you can often walk through the shark tank in an underwater tunnel.

- **Undersea photographers** use special underwater cameras to take pictures of tourists with sharks as part of the experience.

◀ A diver has a close encounter with a great white shark while cage-diving.

Sharks in captivity

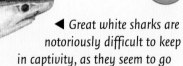

- **Most shark species** are difficult to keep in captivity. They need tanks with lots of space.

- **For a shark to survive** in captivity the water has to have conditions that exactly match the shark's natural habitat.

- **For this reason**, many aquariums only keep sharks that come from their own local area. The further a shark is from home, the harder it is to recreate the conditions it is used to.

- **Sand tiger, lemon sharks and smaller sharks** do better in captivity than other species of shark.

- **Captive sharks** can suffer from diseases such as goitre, caused by a lack of the minerals they need to stay healthy.

- **Sharks in captivity** seem to eat less than those in the wild. In captivity they do not expend so much energy in finding food or in day-to-day living.

◀ Great white sharks are notoriously difficult to keep in captivity, as they seem to go off their food when they are in a tank.

- **The tiger shark** is one of the few large, fierce sharks to have survived a long time in captivity. They have been kept in aquariums for up to five years.

- **To be transported** from the wild to an aquarium, sharks have to be carried in special holding tanks that are transported on trucks or planes.

- **In 1998**, a group of sandbar sharks died in an aquarium in the UK after getting too cold when their flight was delayed at Amsterdam airport.

★ STAR FACT ★
One great white shark kept in an aquarium was so distressed that it kept swimming into the walls of the tanks, and had to be released.

Sharks in trouble

★ STAR FACT ★
Many shark species are so hard to study that scientists have no idea how many of them are left in the sea.

- **There are far fewer sharks** than there used to be. The numbers of many species are falling fast. Some are in danger of dying out.

- **This is mainly because** of human activities such as hunting and fishing.

- **Overfishing** may mean that shark populations can't recover. Porbeagle sharks have been overfished.

- **In the second half of the 20th century,** shark fishing increased as shark meat, shark's-fin soup became more popular.

- **Sharks are also in demand** because other fish such as cod have become scarce, having also been overfished.

- **Many sharks are killed** when they get caught in nets put up to protect swimmers from shark attacks.

- **Sharks caught for sport** are usually released, but often die from exhaustion soon afterwards.

- **Because sharks grow slowly** and don't bear many young, it is especially hard for a species to build up its numbers again after being overfished.

- **Sharks are at the top of the food chain.** Poisonous chemicals from pollution collect in sea creatures. When sharks eat their prey, the poison builds up in their bodies. Scientists think this may make sharks ill and make it harder for them to reproduce.

◀ *Shark pups are very vulnerable while they are in their egg cases, and many do not survive into adulthood. This makes it difficult for shark populations to recover from over-fishing.*

Endangered species

- **An endangered species** is in danger of dying out and becoming extinct.

- **When a species becomes extinct**, all the members of that species die and it can never exist again.

- **Scientists try to find out** if a shark species is at risk by counting the sharks seen in a particular area and measuring how much this changes over time.

- **Experts found** that sandbar shark sightings on America's east coast fell by 20 percent over 20 years. The sandbar shark is now endangered.

- **Well-known sharks** that are endangered include great white, whale and basking sharks.

- **Most sharks** are endangered because of overfishing.

- **International organizations** such as the IUCN (International Union for the Conservation of Nature and Natural Resources) compile lists of which species are endangered.

- **According to the IUCN** over 50 shark species are now endangered.

- **Some sharks and shark relatives** are threatened when natural coastlines and estuaries are developed and built on. This destroys nursery areas where sharks lay eggs or bear their young.

- **The Ganges shark**, found in the river Ganges in India, is one of the most endangered sharks.

◀ *Great whites are one species that are known to be in danger of dying out. There are several international campaigns to try to save them.*

Shark beliefs and folklore

- **Throughout history**, people have believed all sorts of things about sharks. Many unproved shark beliefs still survive to this day.

- **Sailors used to say** sharks could smell a dead body and followed a ship if someone on board had died. Scientists today think this may be true.

- **Sailors also used to believe** that sharks liked eating humans and would go out of their way to find them. In fact, this isn't true at all.

- **In the past**, many peoples around the world worshipped shark gods .

- **People from the Solomon Islands**, in the Pacific Ocean, believed that the spirits of people who had died lived on in sharks.

◀ Sharks are common in the waters around the Pacific island of Fiji. Local people have many beliefs and customs relating to sharks.

- **The Solomon Islanders** even used to make human sacrifices to sharks to keep the shark-spirits happy.

- **In Vietnam**, the whale shark is known as ca ong or 'Sir Fish'. It was once worshipped there .

- **Sharks rarely get diseases**, so many people believe eating shark products can protect against illness. There is no scientific evidence for this.

- **In Fiji in the Pacific Ocean**, people used to catch sharks and kiss their stomachs. This was believed to make the sharks harmless.

- **In Europe**, catching a shark used to be considered good luck, especially if it was female.

Shark myths and legends

- **There are many myths and legends** involving sharks, most of them from places where sharks are common.

- **Hawaiian legends** tell of a shark king and a shark queen who controlled all the other sharks in the sea.

- **In one Hawaiian myth**, a god threw a shark into the sky, where it formed the constellations.

- **In a legend** of the Warrau people of South America, a man arranged for his mother-in-law to be eaten by a shark. As punishment his own leg was bitten off and became the constellation of Orion's Belt.

- **Another Hawaiian story** tells how a shark king married a human woman. They had a son, who grew up to find he could turn himself into a shark.

- **The Bible** tells how the prophet Jonah was swallowed by a 'great fish'. In most translations this is a whale, but some people think it might have meant a shark.

- **The ancient Greek writer Aristotle** developed a theory that sharks had to roll upside-down in order to bite. This isn't true, but the myth lived on for centuries.

- **In legends from the South Pacific**, 'shark men' were sharks that could take human form and come ashore.

- **Old Japanese legends** also featured a terrifying god called the shark man.

▶ Jonah was thought to have been trapped in the belly of the great fish for three days.

★ STAR FACT ★
When China and Japan fought each other in the Second World War, the Chinese painted sharks on their planes to scare the Japanese.

Saving sharks

- **Some sharks are now endangered**, and people have started working to try to save them.

- **Ecotourism** helps to save sharks by encouraging local people not to kill sharks, as they can make money from them as tourist attractions.

- **Some shark-fishing countries** have imposed quotas to limit how many sharks fishermen can catch.

- **Governments** can ban the killing of some sharks altogether. The UK has passed a law making it illegal to catch or disturb a basking shark.

- **Some countries have set up** marine wildlife reserves where harming wildlife is banned.

- **Conservation charities** such as WWF (The WorldWide Fund for Nature) work to educate people to help them avoid killing sharks unnecessarily.

★ STAR FACT ★
Some scientists are worried that diving with sharks makes them less scared of humans, which could put sharks at greater risk.

- **By banning trade** in shark products, governments can stop some people from killing sharks.

- **To help protect sharks**, people should avoid buying products such as shark's-fin soup.

- **Some shark charities** will let you 'adopt' a shark. You pay a fee and receive information about a shark living in a protected area. The money goes towards conservation campaigns.

▼ *Some sharks take an interest in diving cages, and seem to become more tame when they have contact with humans.*

Sharks in art, books and films

- **Ancient peoples** made images of sharks. Maori artists made carvings of sharks from wood and bone.

- **Ancient aboriginal rock art** depict sharks, along with other animals important to the early Aborigines.

- **In 1778**, American artist John Singleton Copley painted a famous picture of Brook Watson being attacked by a shark.

- **In his 1851 novel** *Moby Dick*, Herman Melville described a character almost losing his hand to a shark, even though it had been killed and dragged on board.

- **Another famous novel**, 20,000 *Leagues Under the Sea* by Jules Verne, features man-eating sharks.

- **The best-known shark novel** is *Jaws*, by Peter Benchley, published in 1974. It tells of a great white shark attacking swimmers off the east coast off the USA.

- **In 1975**, *Jaws* was made into a film by Steven Spielberg. It broke box-office records and is still one of the biggest-grossing films of all time.

- **Much of** *Jaws* was filmed using a 7 m-long artificial shark, known as Bruce.

- **There were three film sequels to** *Jaws*, including a 3D version. The audience wore special 3D spectacles that made the shark appear to come out of the screen towards them.

- **In a later shark movie**, *Deep Blue Sea* (1999), the shark sequences were partly created using computer animation.

◀ A still from the shark film Deep Blue Sea. It tells the story of a group of scientists who use genetic engineering to create super-intelligent sharks – which then turn against their captors.

Shark science

- **We know relatively little about sharks.** Scientists are trying to find out more about them.

- **The study of sharks** is sometimes called elasmobranchology.

- **Knowing more about sharks** – things such as how they breed and what they need to survive – will help us to conserve them and stop shark species from dying out.

- **To find out how sharks live**, scientists have to study them in the wild. This is called 'fieldwork'.

- **Scientists also catch sharks** so they can study them in captivity. This lets them look closely at how sharks swim, eat, breed and behave in other ways.

- **In laboratories**, scientists study things such as sharks' blood, skin and cartilage to find out how their bodies work.

- **Some scientists study sharks' cells** to try to find out why they get so few diseases. This information could help to make new medicines.

- **In aquariums**, scientists test sharks' reactions to see how their brains and senses work.

- **Governments and wildlife charities** sometimes pay scientists to study sharks.

▲ Denticles are incredibly hard and strong, but still flexible enough to allow great mobility. Scientists are interested in the possibilities of recreating the effects of denticles for human use.

Shark scientists

- **There are many different types** of scientists who work with sharks.

- **Biologists** are scientists who study living things. Many shark scientists are marine biologists – which means they study sea life.

- **Zoologists** are scientists who study animals, and ichthyologists are scientists who study fish. These scientists also work with sharks.

- **Other scientists** study shark genes and DNA – the instructions inside cells. Scientists who study genes and DNA are called geneticists.

- **Palaeontologists** study fossils. Shark fossils are very important in revealing how sharks evolved. Some scientists specialize in studying just shark fossils.

- **Oceanographers** study the sea. They know about habitats and how sharks live with other animals.

◀ This diver is wearing the latest diving equipment. This allows scientists to study sharks close-up in their natural habitats.

- **Most shark scientists** work for universities or research centres such as the Woods Hole Oceanographic Institute in Massachusetts, USA.

- **One of today's most famous shark scientists** is American zoologist Dr. Eugenie Clark. She has studied shark behaviour and deep-sea sharks.

- **The famous French undersea expert** Jacques Cousteau was one of the first people to study sharks underwater. He invented scuba diving equipment, which scientists still use when studying sharks.

- **If you'd like to be a shark scientist**, it will help if you pick subjects such as biology and chemistry at school, and study biology or zoology at university.

Studying sharks

- **To learn more about sharks**, scientists need ways of finding, following and catching them.

- **Most shark scientists** have to be strong and good at diving.

- **Scientists** often use diving cages or protective chainmail suits to get close to sharks.

- **They can also study sharks** such as great whites without going in the water, using cameras on the ends of long poles.

- **To follow sharks**, scientists radio-track them. They catch a shark and attach a transmitter that gives out radio signals. Wherever the shark goes, they can pick up the signals and work out the shark's location.

- **Some shark scientists** dissect dead sharks to find out about their bodies or what they have eaten recently.

◀ Studies of reef sharks often begin by tracking mature females to gain data on breeding times and to locate habitat sites for newborn pups.

- **Scientists tag sharks** by attaching a tag saying where and when the shark was last seen. The same shark may then be found again somewhere else, giving scientists clues about shark movements.

- **A camera** can be attached to a shark to record its travels. The strap holding the camera gradually dissolves, and the camera floats to the surface to be collected.

- **To tag or track a shark**, scientists have to catch it using a net or trap. They may drug it so that they can attach the transmitter or tag safely.

- **Scientists have to be careful** when working with live sharks, as they may get bitten by a shark that is not happy about being caught.

Early sharks

- **Sharks first evolved** about 380 million years ago. That means they were around long before the dinosaurs.

- **Sharks' basic body shapes** and behaviour have hardly changed since they first appeared.

- **Experts think sharks evolved** from ancient types of fish that had no jawbones.

- **Sharks appeared** long before many other kinds of fish that are alive today, such as salmon and goldfish.

- **One of the earliest sharks of all** was *Cladoselache*, which lived 370 million years ago. It was around 1.5 m long, and had 3-pointed teeth, just as frilled sharks do now.

- *Stethacanthus*, which lived about 350 million years ago, was a strange-looking shark with a platform of denticles on top of its first dorsal fin.

◄ A fossilized *Megalodon* tooth (left) compared to a tooth from a modern great white shark.

- *Hybodus* **lived about 160 million years ago**. Like many modern sharks, it had both sharp cutting teeth and flat, blunt, chewing teeth.

- **The biggest shark ever** was probably *Megalodon*. It first appeared about 20 million years ago. Scientists think it looked like a great white shark, only bigger –maybe 20 m in length (as long as two buses).

- **Of course**, these prehistoric sharks didn't have these names when they were alive, as there were no humans around to name them. Their names have been given to them by modern scientists.

- **Sharks survived** a huge mass extinction 65 million years ago, which wiped out other creatures such as dinosaurs and ammonites.

Shark fossils

- **A fossil is a record** of the shape of an animal, or part of an animal, preserved in rock.

- **A fossil forms** when an animal dies and is gradually covered by earth. Over a very long time, the sand or mud hardens into rock. The animal rots away, but its shape is left behind, and may get filled in with minerals to leave a 'model' of the animal.

- **Often**, only the hardest parts of an animal, such as its skeleton, get fossilized.

- **Because sharks have soft cartilage skeletons**, there are few whole shark fossils. Many shark fossils only show teeth or fins.

- **Scientists use shark fossils** to find out what sharks looked like long ago and how they lived. They often use tooth fossils to guess how big an entire shark was.

- **Shark fossils are often found** on land in places that used to be seas millions of years ago.

- **Some of the best shark fossil areas** are in parts of the USA, such as California, Maryland and Oklahoma.

- **Palaeontologists** go searching for fossils at sites and dig, cut or chip them out of the rocks. Then they take them back to a lab to clean them and study them.

- **Fossils show** that some sharks that are alive today are very similar to ones that lived millions of years ago.

- **Fossils are often displayed** at museums and fossil shops.

◄ A palaeontologist at work. They have to be very careful when they dig delicate fossils out of the ground.

Shark discoveries and mysteries

- **Shark scientists** are still finding out new things about sharks, and puzzling over unanswered questions.

- **Shark experts** sometimes disagree strongly about shark facts. They meet up at conferences where they share their discoveries and hold debates.

- **For example**, some experts think the prehistoric shark *Megalodon* died out over a million years ago, while others say it lived until 10,000 years ago.

- **No one knows** why basking sharks seem to disappear at certain times of year.

- **The dwarf lanternshark** was discovered in 1985. New species of sharks are still being found.

- **Scientists don't always find new shark species** in the sea. Instead, they are often found in fish markets or reported by local people.

- **In 2004**, scientists found that Greenland sharks eat giant squid. Before this, only sperm whales were thought to eat these creatures.

- **In 2002**, scientists worked out how to test the DNA in shark's-fin soup to see which species it contains. This helps to stop people hunting protected sharks.

- **Scientists studying whale sharks** found that they don't just eat plankton. Sometimes they wait for other fish to lay their eggs so that they can eat them.

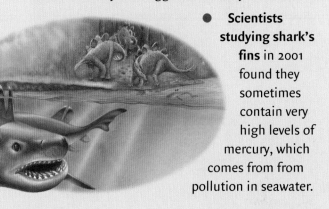

- **Scientists studying shark's fins** in 2001 found they sometimes contain very high levels of mercury, which comes from from pollution in seawater.

▲ *Most of what we know about prehistoric sharks such as* Hybodus *comes from studying the fossilized remains of their teeth.*

Shark records

- **The most widespread shark** is the blue shark, found in most of the world's seas and oceans.

- **The brightest luminescent shark** is the cookie-cutter. Its glow is as bright as a reading lamp.

- **More than ten shark species** share the title of rarest shark, as they are known from only one specimen. They include two types of angel shark, the Taiwan angel shark and the ocellated angel shark.

- **The flattest-bodied sharks** are angel and wobbegong sharks.

- **The bigeye thresher shark** has the biggest eyes in relation to its body size than any other shark.

◀ *The great white shark is the largest of the predatory sharks.*

- **The shortfin mako** makes the highest leaps. It can jump more than 5 m out of the water.

- **The whale shark** has the most pups at once – as many as 300.

- **The fussiest eaters of the shark world** are bullhead 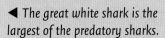 sharks. The diet of some bullheads consists of just sea urchins.

- **The common thresher shark** has the longest tail compared to its body size.

- **The great white shark** has had more books written and films made about it than any other shark.

INDEX

Entries in **bold** refer to main subject entries. Entries in *italics* refer to illustrations.

A

adoption 56
aggression 21, 28, 32
air 14, 28
anatomy 6, 8, *8*, 20
ampullae of Lorenzini **13**, *13*, 25, 35
angel shark 6, 19, **43**, *43*, 53, 61
  diet 16
  as food 43, 48
aquariums 28, 35, 41, 52, **54**
Aristotle 20, 48, 56
art 58
attacks 26, 28, 31, 32, 33, 35, 40, 41, 48, **49**, **50–51**
  biting 34, 41, 51, 52, 59
  hitting with tails 27
  risk of 6, 12, 29, 42, **49**, **51**, **52**

B

baby sharks *see* pups
bait 17
balance 11
barbels **11**, 40, 41, 44
barbelthroat carpet shark 40
barnacles 23
barndoor skate 47
basking shark **29**, 51, 52, *52*, 61
  diet 17
  risk of extinction 55
batoids 45, 46–47
beliefs about sharks 56
benthic shark 24
bigeye thresher shark 27, 61
biggest shark 7, 29
bigmouth shark *see* basking shark
bioluminescence 10, **18**, 21, 37, 61
birth 22
black-tip reef shark (black shark) 33, *33*
black-tip shark (spinner shark) **33**
blind electric ray 46
blind shark 41, *41*
blood 8
blue pointer shark *see* mako shark

blue shark 24, **32**, *32*, 61
  mating areas 20
  migrations and travel 25, 32, 61
blue whale 17
bluegray carpet shark *see* blind shark
body language 21
bone shark *see* basking shark
bones 8, 45
bonito shark *see* mako shark
bonnethead shark (bonnet shark *or* bonnetnose shark) **34**, *34*, 35
bony fish 8, 45
brain *8*, 12, 13
bramble shark 38, *38*
breathing 11, **14**, 41, 46
bull shark 19, 24, **32**, *32*, 35, 49, 51
  diet 16
bullhead shark 21, 61

C

cage-diving 11, *11*, 54, *54*, 56
cameras 48, 54, 59
camouflage 19, 31, 40, 43
  for divers 51
carpet shark 13, 16, **40–41**, 42, *40*, *41*, *42*
  skin 53
catshark *8*, *8*, 45, 53
cartilage **8**, *8*, 45, 53
cartilaginous fish 8, 45
catshark 21, **36**
caudal fins 9
chain shark 36
charities 55, 56, 58
chemicals 11, 51, 55, 61
chimaera 45, **48**, *48*
cigar shark *see* spined pygmy shark
Cladoselache 60
Clark, Eugenie 59
classification 25
cleaning 17, 23
Colcough's shark *see* blind shark
colour 18, 19
colour vision 10
common skate 47, *47*
common thresher shark 27, 61
communication 18, 21
companions 23

conservation
  campaigns and charities 55, 56
cookie-cutter shark 19, **39**, *39*, 61
co-operation 23
copepods 23, 37
Copley, John Singleton 58
coral reefs 24, *24*
Cousteau, Jacques 59
crocodile shark **30**, *30*

D

danger *see* attacks
Deep Blue Sea (film) 58, *58*
defence 18, 19
denticles **9**, 58, *58*
diet 6, 7, 15, **16**, 17, 22, 39
disguise 19
  see also camouflage
disease 54, 55, 57, 58
dissection 59
diving 33, 40, *40*, 41, 51, **59**
  cage-diving 11, *11*, 54, *54*, 56
  spear-fishing 28
DNA testing 61
dogfish shark 10, 18, 21, 36, **37**, *37*, 39
  as danger 51
  diet 16
  tagging 25, *25*
  travel 25
dogfish shark, prickly 38
dogshark 36
dogshark, dwarf 38
dolphins 54
dominance 34
dorsal fins 9, 35, 45
draughtboard shark 36
droppings 8
dwarf dogshark 38
dwarf lanternshark 7, 61

E

ears 11
eating habits 16, 17, 44
ecotourism 54, 56
egg cases 21, *21*, 42, 43, 47, 48
eggs 21, 22, 25
electric ray 45, *45*, 46
electricity and electrical detection **13**, 21, 29, 31, 35, 46

elephant shark *see* basking shark
endangered species 55, 56, 61
epaulette shark 9, 19, 24, 25, 40
experiments 12, 13, 35, 41, 58
extinction 55, 56, 60
eyes 10, *10*

F

false catshark 36
families (classification of types) 25
feeding frenzy 16, 32
fiction 58
  see also myths
films 49, **58**
filter-feeding 16, **17**, 42, 46
fins 8, **9**, *9*, 14, 37
  see also shark's-fin soup
fish
  bones 8
  cartilage 8
  lateral line 11
  relatives of sharks 6, 45, 46–47, 48
  scales 9
fishing 28, 32, 37, 48, **52**, 55, 56
  as sport 26, 52, 55
food 6, 7, 15, **16**, 17, 22, 23, 39
  sharks as 26, 32, 37, 43, 44, **52**, **53**, 55 (*see also* shark's-fin soup)
flexibility 8
food chain 55
fossils 45, 59, **60**
fresh water 24, 32
frilled shark 45
frilled wobbegong shark 40

G

Galapagos shark 24
Ganges shark 24, 55
ghost shark 48
gill rakers 17
gill slits **14**, *14*, 45, 48
gills 14
glowing *see* luminescence
goblin shark 25, **29**, *29*
governments 56, 58
grayfish 53
great hammerhead shark 35

great white shark 6, 7, *12*, *16*, 19, **26**, *26*, *49*, *50*, *51*, 55, 61
  attacks by and fear of 26, 49, 50, 51
  in captivity 26, 54
  diet 16, 17
  olfactory lobe 12
  risk of extinction 55
  scavenging 17
  senses 12
  skeleton *8*
  teeth 15, *18*, *26*
green dogfish shark 18
green sawfish 47
Greenland shark **37**, *37*, 48, 53
  diet 17, 61
  habitat 24, 39
grey nurse shark *see* sand tiger shark
group 19, 21, 29, 35, 37
growth 20, 22, 55
  rings 22
guitarfish 19
gummy shark 36
gums 15
gurry shark *see* Greenland shark

H

habitat 6, **24**, **25**, 32, 33, 37
hakari 53
hammerhead shark 6, *6*, 9, *13*, *16*, 19, 24, *24*, **34**, **35**, *34*, *35*
  diet 16
  intelligence 13
  reproduction 22
  social systems 13, 34
hearing 11
heart 8, *8*
Herodotus 48
hiding 18, 43
hitching 23
homes *see* habitat
hooktooth shark 36
horn shark 10, 24, **43**, *43*, 51
houndshark 36
humans
  as danger to sharks 18, 32, 48, 52, 55, 56
  contact with sharks 52, 54, 56, 57
  uses of sharks 29, 36, 37, 43, 48, 52, **53**

hunting 16, 28, 38
huss 53
Hybodus 60, **61**, 61
hygiene 17, 23

I

intelligence 13, 41
IUCN (International
Union for the
Conservation of
Nature and Natural
Resources) 55

J

Japanese angel shark
43
Japanese saw shark
44
Jaws (book/film) 49,
58
jewellery 43, 53
Jonah 56, *56*

K

krill 29, *29*

L

lanternshark 18, *18*
lanternshark, dwarf 7,
61
large-tooth cookie-
cutter shark 39
large-tooth sawfish
47
lateral line 11, *11*
Latin names 25, 30
laws 56
leather 37, 53, *53*
leeches 23
legends 56
lemon shark **13**, 19,
35, *35*, 36, 54
leopard shark 19, **36**,
36
life span 22, 42
light 10, 19
see also
luminescence
liver 8, *8*, 29, 36, 53
lollipop catshark 36
long-tailed carpet shark
40
longfin mako shark 26
longnose saw shark
44
Lorenzini, Stefano 13
Lorenzini, ampullae of
13, 25, 35
luminescence 10, **18**,
21, 37, 61
lungs 14

M

mackerel shark 25, 26
see also porbeagle
shark
magnetism 25
mako shark 14, **26**,
26, 61
mangrove stingray 46
manta ray 45, 46, *46*,
51
marine wildlife
reserves 56
mating 18, 19, **20**, 25,
35
medicinal uses 53
Megalodon 7, 60, 61
megamouth shark 17,
30, *30*
Melville, Herman 58
mercury 61
'mermaids' purses' 21
migration **25**, 32, 38
vertical 25, 38
Moby Dick 58
monkfish *see* angel
shark
migration **25**, 32, 38
movement 9, 14
muscles 8, *8*
Muslims 53
myths 56

N

navigation 25
necklaces 53
nerves and nerve
endings 11
nostrils 12
number of species 6
nurse shark 19, 24,
24, **41**, *41*, 42
attacks by 41, 51
diet 16
mating areas 20
nurse shark, grey *see*
sand tiger shark
nursery areas 22, 24

O

oceanic white-tip shark
33
oceans, cleaning 17
oil 29, 36, 37, 53
orders 25
organs 8, *8*
oscellated angel shark
61
overfishing 55
oviparous sharks 21,
22
ovoviviparous sharks
22
oxygen 14

P

parasites 23
parenting 19, 21, 22
pectoral fins 9, 14
pelagic sharks 24
pelagic thresher shark
27
pelvic fins 14
pharmaceutical
products 36, 53
pheromones 20, 21
photography 48, 54,
59
photophores 18
piked dogfish shark 37
pilot fish 23
pineal eye 10
plankton 17
poisons 55, 61
pollution 11, 55, 61
porbeagle shark 19,
28, *28*, 55
Port Jackson shark 14,
21, 43
Portuguese shark 24
precaudal pit 36
predators of sharks
18, 22
see also humans
pregnancy 45
prehistoric sharks 10,
45, **60**, 61
prickly dogfish shark
38
prickly sharks 38
pups (young sharks)
19, 21, **22**, 24
pygmy shark 7, 10, 25,
38, *38*, 52

R

radio-tracking 59
ragged-tooth shark *see*
sand tiger shark
ratfish 48, *48*
rays (fish) 6, 10, 44,
45, **47**, *46*, *47*
recycling 17
relatives 6, 45, 46–47,
48, 60
remora 23
reproduction **20**, **21**,
22, 55
requiem shark 32
research 22, 25, 45,
58, 59, 60–61
see also experiments
reserves 56
river stingray 46
rock salmon *see* spiny
dogfish shark
rostrums and rostral
teeth 44
round stingray 46

S

safety 51
sailors 49, 57
sand devil *see* angel
shark
sand tiger shark (sand
shark) 15, 22, 25,
28, *28*, 54
sandbar shark 54, 55
sandpaper 9, 43
saw shark 9, 10, **44**,
44, 47
saw shark, six-gill 45
sawfish 10, 44, 45,
47, *47*
scales 9
scalloped hammerhead
shark 13, *13*, 35
scavenging 17, 37
school *see* group
science 22, 25, 45,
58, 59, 60–61
see also experiments
scientific names 25,
30
scuba divers 33
sea leeches 23
sea water 24
oxygen content 14
sealife centres 35, 52,
54
sealion 51, 54
seal 49, 51
seaweed 21, 24
senses **10**, **11**, **12**, **13**,
16, 44, 51, 57
sensing electricity **13**,
21, 29, 31, 35
see also electricity
and electrical
detection
seven-gill shark 45
shagreen 9, 43, 53
shape **6**, 14
shark screens 51
shark sucker 23
sharks
study of 20, 48, 52,
55, **58**, **59** (*see
also* science)
young *see* pups
shark's-fin soup 9, 36,
53, 55, 56, 61
sharkwatching 17
shoal *see* group
short-nose electric ray
46
shortfin mako shark
14, 26, *26*, 61
shovelhead *see*
bonnethead shark
shovelnose shark 19
shy-eye shark 10, 36
sicklefin weasel shark
36

sight 10
silky shark *14*, *25*
silvertip shark *19*, *23*
single-sex groups 19
six-gill saw shark 45
six-gill shark 45
sixth sense 13
see also electricity
and electrical
detection
size 6, **7**
skates (fish) 45, **47**,
47
skeleton **8**, *8*, 45
skin **9**, 18, 20, 38, *38*,
42
sleeper shark *see*
Greenland shark
slime shark *see* pygmy
shark
smell, sense of 12,
16, 44, 51, 57
smooth dogfish shark
17
smooth hammerhead
shark 13, *13*, 35
smooth hound shark
15
snaggletooth shark 36
snout 6, *10*, 44, 51
social systems 13, **19**,
20, **21**, 34
soup, shark-fin 9, 36,
53, 55, 56, 61
soupfin shark 36
species 6, 25
endangered 55, 56,
61
speed 14, 32
Spielberg, Steven 58
spikes and spines **10**,
10, 18, 38, *38*, 43,
51
spined pygmy shark 7,
10, 25, **38**, *38*
spine (backbone) 8, *8*
spinner shark (black-tip
shark) **33**
spiny dogfish shark 10,
37, 53
spiracles 11, 14, 41,
46
spitting shark 42
spookfish 48
sport, fishing as 26,
52, 55
spotted eagle ray 46,
46
spotted wobbegong
shark 53
squalene 53
steering 9, 12
Stethacanthus 60
stingray 10, 35, 46, 51
stomach 8, *8*

sunfish *see* basking shark
superstition 49, 57
surfing 49
survival rate 22
swallowing air 14, 28
swell shark 18, 21, 36
swim bladder 14
swimmers (human) 9, 33, 49, 51, 52
swimming with sharks 54
symbiosis 23

T

tagging 25, 59
tail 8, **9**, 14, 46
Taiwan angel shark 61
tanks, sharks in 28, 35, 41, 52, **54**
tapetum lucidum 10

tapeworm 23
tasselled wobbegong shark 40
taste, sense of 11, 16, 44
tawny shark 42
teeth **15**, *15*, 22, 44, 45
  rostral 44
  uses by humans 37, 48, 53
territory 24
Texas skate 47
third eye 10
thresher shark 9, 18, **27**, *27*, 61
  tail 9, 18, 27, 42, 61
tiger shark 13, 28, **31**, *31*, 32, 35, 49, 54
  eyes 10, *10*
  pups 22
  teeth 15, *15*
tope shark 36

touch, sense of 11, 44
tourism 54, 56
tracking 25, 59
training 13, 54
transporting 54
travel 24, 25, 32
tuna 6

V

velvet belly shark 18
Verne, Jules 58
vertical migration 25, 38
vibrations 11
vision 10
vitamin pills 53
vitamin shark 36
viviparous sharks 22, 43
vomiting 17, 18, 49

W

weapons 46, 48, 51
weasel shark **36**, *36*
weight 8, 14
whale shark 7, *7*, *17*, 19, 25, 40, *40*, **42**, *42*, 52
  diet 17, 42, 61
  reproduction 22, 61
  risk of extinction 55
whales 7, 17
  sharks scavenging 17, 37
whiskers *see* barbels
whiskery shark 36
white-tip reef shark 14, *14*, *20*, **33**, *33*
  habitat 24, 33
  social systems 19, 20
  territory 24
wildlife charities 55, 56, 58

wildlife reserves 56
winghead shark 35
wobbegong shark (wobbies) **40**, *40*, 42, 51, 53, 61
  camouflage 19, 40, 43
wrasse 23
WWF (The World Wide Fund for Nature) 56

Z

zebra shark 19, 21, **42**, *42*, 52